Beyond All Things

Insights to Awaken Joy, Purpose, and Spiritual Connection

Dr. Azriela Jankovic

BEYOND ALL THINGS
Insights to Awaken Joy, Purpose, and Spiritual Connection

ISBN: 978-0-578-58023-4

www.azrielajankovic.com

Table of Contents

This book is dedicated to each and every one of you...
For the good that you do in this world... even when nobody is looking.

Introduction

Who is wise?
One who learns from all.
—Pirkei Avot

I n our midst of more conveniences and material abundance than in any other period of history, we are beginning to understand that happiness – true and lasting joy and purpose – is not the product of our material surroundings alone. It is only through the process of reawakening and connecting authentically with the often-hidden depths both around us and within us that our lives can blossom in fullness.

Searching for depth and meaning in years past may have led a person to any number of religious institutions. Right now, as you are reading these words, a growing number of young people are choosing something new and different.[1] For the first time in human history, we are afforded access to information and inspiration from every corner of the world. We are converging together and beginning to recognize the great Spiritual Truths that unite all of humanity.

We may ask, why are we here? What is our purpose? What is our place within this vast universe? Together, we will set out to answer these questions. We will answer them with ideas and information, and by creating a personal connection, awareness, and understanding of Truth that can only arise through our experience.

In every moment, we have a unique opportunity to access the deepest parts of ourselves and feel connected to all of creation. As of our mode of operation in the modern world has peaked in its complexity, spirituality beckons to remind us there is beauty and serenity in simplicity. There is peace and wholeness in the present moment.

The fifty insights in this book are intended to provide inspiration and guidance on your way. The accompanying reflections provide you with an opportunity to experience and internalize what you're learning and discovering.

One thought, one word, or one action has the power to change your life and in turn, this world.

One

Connecting with Radiance

Jerusalem, 2003

The crisp, chilly, early morning winds whipped through white stone corridors and alleyways as I walked with determination toward an old building, home to a collection of spiritual books.

I was twenty-three years old, newly married. My husband and I had ventured across the globe to delve into the world of ancient spirituality and seek out truth. My quest for answers had, so far, only yielded more questions, and I continued to search.

Arriving in Jerusalem, I knew that the answers were not far off. Yet it felt as though they were hiding in the crevices between the ancient stones, and that in order to access them, I'd need to do some strategic digging.

During my first weeks, while visiting learning institutions where I had the opportunity to ask my most pressing question, I was left feeling fractured by the details of how to practice what, and which way, and according to whom.

"Where is my place in this world?" I asked, as I knew, deep within, that spirituality could help me connect more deeply to all of life… if only I could figure out how to practice it in sincerity.

Growing up, my happy place had always been a book shop. With a cappuccino in one hand and a book in the other, most weekends found me engrossed in myriad books about spirituality and personal growth. First, it was Barnes and Noble. Next, it was a part-time job in high school working at a psychic bookstore, researching the deeper world, and quelling my inner skeptic while secretly wondering if the psychics could read my mind. Next, it was the university library for an exploration of world culture, sociology, religion, and philosophy.

On this particular morning, my journey had led me into a Jerusalem institute of spiritual learning and its library of ancient books. Perusing a collection stretched floor to ceiling, I brushed up against a shelf, and one book broke loose and cascaded down onto my head. With light blue skies and wispy clouds, the cover drew me in.

Awestruck, I opened it and began to read.

Within moments, a young woman rushed through the door. Hair blown by the wind, she looked as if she had just run a marathon. "There is an older woman who needs assistance," she announced. "She just had surgery and she's alone in her home until her children arrive from the States." Within many of Jerusalem's institutes of learning, you will find a three-pronged focus for spiritual growth: learning, prayer, and performing acts of kindness. When a neighbor is in need, students mobilize to volunteer. "I'll go," I answered, and gently closed the book. "What's her name? Where does she live?"

"Ruchoma Shain, two streets south." As she answered, I glanced down at the book in my hands and realized that the author of my book was this very same woman in need of help. I rushed out the door.

T here are certain moments in life that feel completely outside of the laws of nature. In moments such as these, when people meet, and lives collide, one begins to wonder about the chances of these occurrences taking place. The chances seem so slim that they border the impossible. What were the chances of *that one book* falling from its shelf?

That moment, sixteen years ago, was a distinct coincidence of time and space.

It was a moment that led me to a warm, caring teacher who had amassed a lifetime of experience and was delighted to share her wisdom with me. She was able to shine a light on the answers to some of my deepest questions: *Why are we here?*

How can we create a joyful, vibrant, and meaningful life?

It was a moment, which in fact, led me to many more 'coincidences' of its kind.

As has been said, when the student is ready, the teacher appears.

During my time in Jerusalem, I began to discover wellsprings of deep ancient wisdom: how and where to find truth, how to feel spiritually connected, and how to imbue or find purpose in the present moment. This exploration was an introduction to a prolific world of ancient spirituality. Its teachings hold the keys to Oneness with all of life.

In this book, I will share my journey with you, along with insights and ideas that I've been collecting along the way. Perhaps you are reading this book to learn more about an ancient type of spiritual, personal, and collective development. Or, perhaps you are hoping to further transcend the aches and pains of daily living. You have heard the whispers of your soul, and you are listening intently.

What is it that you would like to learn or receive from a collection of ancient insights and soul-stirring stories? If your soul could speak to you, what might it say? This book was written for you. It is an opportunity to tune in with your most authentic self and to answer the calling of your soul by channeling spirituality into being by way of your thoughts, words, and acts. My journey led to the universe of Torah. Torah is the original Hebrew word for the Five Books of Moses and its related philosophies, legal code, commentaries, and deep, hidden spiritual teachings. The word "Torah" is connected to the Hebrew word "Ho-rah-ah," which means 'guidance.' This guidance is a wellspring of wisdom from which one can draw from at any moment. While it is traditionally associated with the ancient Hebrews, so many of its teachings are universal.

No matter your background, the Universal Truth of Torah can carry you into a spiritually rich life. The world has been created and is constantly being sustained and supervised by a Great Being that is both *beyond* and *within* all things.

Our ability to communicate an understanding of this Being is limited by the confines of our sensory perception and linguistic or physical expression. The Torah describes this Being in anthropomorphic descriptions, because the Torah speaks to humans, and so it speaks the language of humans. Yet, it also explains that this Being has no body or form, which leaves room for a more personal, relational experience with It, which will be experienced as uniquely as each and every human being has been created.

The Hebrew language uses many names to describe The Being, in a way, referring to Its different qualities. In this book, this Being is referred to as "The Infinite," based on the mystical Hebrew name for the Being, "Ein Sof," which means "Without End."

Take a moment to contemplate the notion of having no end. What does it mean to be infinite? Awaken your curiosity, and you may begin to wonder: How can we understand infinity? How can we begin to understand this existence?

P erhaps, the knowledge that we cannot know is one pathway to wisdom.

When we begin to contemplate what it means to be infinite, our minds expand outward into the universe. Our viewpoint begins to encompass all that exists within the realm of space, until we cannot conceptualize its end.

In ancient Hebrew, the word for universe is "Olam," directly related to the word "ne-eh-lam" which means "concealed." All that we experience in the spacial, physical plane, is by nature, a concealment of a spiritual reality that exists both beyond and within everything. This is where The Infinite One lies: beyond, and within all things.

In seeking to connect with the Infinite, we discover and engage with the deeper world both within and around us. We uncover an abundant love and cultivate a personal relationship with the Infinite Oneness of which we are a part.

Let us begin.

Insight # 1: You are a Deep Soul

It may seem that the world of spirituality and depth is outside of your reach. Living in the physical world can feel like an obstacle to serenity. Yet, so much of daily living – even if you don't realize it – may hold the key to your personal transformation.

What is the first human action we perform upon entering this world? We breathe. Breathing, although involuntary, can alter our states of mind. Breathing mindfully, at any moment, can bring about a sense of calm and peace. It enables more carbon dioxide to enter the blood, relaxes the anxious response in the brain, and synchronizes the heartbeat with the breath.[1]

In Hebrew, the word for breath (ne - shee - mah) shares the same root as the word for soul (ne - shah - mah).

We all breathe the same air. It is the same air that has been cycling around our planet since the beginning of time.

Visualize the air around you for a moment and notice how it flows inside of your lungs, throughout your body, and then cycles back out into the world. Picture the living creations that are connected through this cycle – human beings, animals, and plants of all types.

If physical matter were to become invisible so that we would only see the air, we would notice that we are connected, in all moments, to all of creation, by way of breath.

Noticing this connectivity, imagine an invisible thread running through all of life, linking us in ways which we cannot physically sense. This thread is an invisible spiritual connection that flows around us and within us. When we move, even in seemingly small ways, it moves.

According to the Torah, the Infinite breathed life into the first living human being of all time.[2] This required a deep breath. As such, we have been infused with the depths of the Infinite.

Before we need anything else, we need breath. Before we are anything else, we are souls. Our breath can connect us with our souls.

Breathe in… deeply, slowly, and sit with that breath filling your depths. Close your eyes and hear the words in your mind: *I am a deep soul.* Gradually, release the breath.

In every moment, we breathe, and we can choose to notice and focus upon that breath. Life can be happening all around us, and we can be meditatively focused on our that which we choose. No matter what we are experiencing in any given moment, we have the capacity to choose what we will focus on and where we will place our thoughts.

We may not be able to step away and meditate at any moment, but we can take a slow breath and feel the air moving through us. As we slow down and breathe mindfully, we can remind ourselves of our deep connectivity with all of life, and our capacity to choose what we will hold in our minds.

Grow Your Insight # 1

As you breathe, turn your attention to the feeling of breath entering your body. How does it feel to pause and notice your breath? Reflect.

Insight #2: We are One

What is it that unites us as living beings on this planet? What unites us may often seem concealed by distinction. Each fingerprint and each face presents itself uniquely so that no two of us are identical in appearance. We are made of physical matter encapsulating our souls, creating an apparent separation between each one of us and our surroundings. These separations have not always existed. They are distinctions in the physical world.

Mystical Torah teaches that the first human being was a body of spiritual light energy.[3] This original being was much more than a physical body. It encompassed all souls that have ever lived and all the souls that will ever live.

Imagine a spiritual state of being in which the souls of all time were bound into one entity and experienced complete empathy and wholeness with one another. It was a comfortable and safe place to be, yet without being clothed in earthly bodies, the souls could not experience the struggle or fulfillment of physical existence.

Think of a fetus in utero. How comfortable and safe it feels within the confines of its mother, existing in a state of pure, perfect, all-encompassing security. And yet, it cannot experience free choice, self-expression, or independence.

Today, it appears as though we are living life as individuals, separate from one another. Since I exist in a body disconnected from you, we are separated by physicality, the vehicle through which our souls can experience life on this planet. Our bodies enable our souls to create, destroy, and exercise free choice.

In many ways, we are one soul disguised as billions, according to the mystical view of humanity, deeply connected spiritually and emotionally. Each one of us contains a spark of that original light-soul bundle. That is why when we connect authentically with others, we are connecting the sparks.

Within the physical plane, neurochemistry demonstrates our human emotional connectivity. Eye contact, human touch, body language, and verbal communication stimulate measurable physiological responses in the human body. We can view this as a physical representation of our spiritual connectedness.

How could our lives be different if we were to remain mindful of our spiritual and emotional connectedness with all people? What if we were to focus solely upon what we can learn from and share with each person that we meet?

Wisdom comes when we learn from everyone in our lives. In each meeting, we are encountering a spark of the original body of souls… and when we seek that spark, we will uncover it. In focusing on that which unites us, we can move closer to existing in harmony with everyone.

Grow Your Insight # 2

Take a moment to reflect upon meeting someone who attracted you. What have you learned from this person's presence?

Insight # 3: Spiritual Beings in Physical Bodies

We can appreciate the gifts of living in a physical body and celebrate the uniqueness of each fingerprint, reminding us that each spark of light – each soul – is uniquely designed in perfection.

There is a greater Oneness of which we are a part. Each one of us is unique, and yet we share the human experience – a wide range of emotions and thoughts.

As souls moving through this universe in physical bodies, we are seeking connectivity and yet simultaneously drawn to notice distinctions. Our physical bodies and our thoughts may be drawn to that which makes us different, distinct, and unique. Yet, our souls long to reunite with the original soul wherein we are One.

When we seek out and notice threads of connectivity in our lives and find the common, shared experiences and emotions between us, sparks fly.

As we are able to peel back the layers of what separates us superficially and notice what we share on deeper levels, we increase our ability to feel connected with all of life.

Grow Your Insight # 3

When you meet someone this week,
seek out what you have in common.

Insight # 4: Interconnected Souls

It may not feel easy to cultivate harmony with ourselves or with the souls around us. Yes, we are one soul. Yet, the physical world of distinctions is doing everything in its power – its limited power- to convince us otherwise.

Just as words fall short of describing our souls, they are inadequate in accurately describing what it is that has created us. In our attempt to describe and communicate our understandings of the Infinite, and even by way of naming 'It,' we are utilizing or creating limitations that do not exist.

Although the Infinite has created and sustained the universe and lies beyond the realm of our human comprehension, it is brought forth by Torah that everything is within the Infinite; that there is a spark of the Infinite within all of creation. The Infinite One is formless. Simultaneously, everything that we can possibly conceptualize is within It. With this in mind, how could our worldview evolve?

Every particle in the universe — from every soul that lives, every soul that has departed, every blade of grass, every ray of sunshine and every star in the sky are all, collectively, part of The Infinite.

Focusing on this Ultimate Oneness can serve as a powerful anchor to enhance our awareness. We can consider and internalize the miracle of each living being around us, by delving deeply into science, or even by looking closely at a flower. We can slow down and marvel at the wonders of creation. There is a miracle existing in every moment.

Children know this naturally. Recently, one evening when I was cooking dinner, my two-year-old son toddled into the kitchen, giddy with excitement at the sight of steam rising from a boiling pot on the stove. "Wow! Wow! Wow!" he exclaimed.

I noticed my own thought in reaction, "Why are you so excited? It's just a pot of water boiling on the stove." Yet, I did not allow this thought to leave my mind. Silently, I stood beside him, and we both observed hot water evaporating into thin air, watching the steam rising up. I began to notice the subtle shapes and colors, as the vapor wafted and curled, mingling with the sun rays pouring through the kitchen window and highlighting its hues. My son, in his innocence, was teaching me to step out of my mind and into the beauty of the present moment.

It is not difficult to become so immersed in the busy-ness of daily living that we overlook beauty and wonder surrounding us in all moments. How often do we pause to notice that we are existing in a profoundly beautiful universe?

In fact, we are an integral part of this natural world, inextricably connected to the earth, sky, waters, and living organisms. Reconnecting with the natural world can renew our sense of self, and at least a peek into the grandiosity of spiritual wonder that enrobes us in all moments.

Humans are biologically aligned with nature. Immersion in the wilderness boosts our creative problem-solving ability.[4] Nature has a mentally cleansing effect. After two hours of walking through forests, we experience physiological improvements in blood pressure, nervous system activity, and mood states.[5]

Knowing that we undergo physiological changes when immersed in nature can remind us of our interconnectivity with all of life and all of the Infinite.

Grow Your Insight # 4

Seek out an opportunity to connect with nature. Immerse yourself in a park, forest, or ocean, or simply take a moment to examine a plant or flower closely. Reflect.

Insight # 5: Listening to Connect

We are wired for connection with the natural world because we are a part of it. Listening is a tremendously powerful tool to sharpen our connection. It is the cornerstone of our relationships, of our ability to cooperate, and ultimately, of our potential to peacefully coexist.

Once there was a man who was granted one wish. He was given the choice of tremendous wealth, power, or a listening heart. For this wise man the choice was clear: he would choose the listening heart. As a reward for his thoughtful selection, he was also granted tremendous wealth and power.[6]

That man's name was Solomon. Since he chose to have a heart that listens, he evolved into the wisest human of all time. The Infinite knew that if Solomon had a listening heart and could understand others with true empathy, he could handle the great responsibilities that accompany both immense wealth and kingship. The ability to listen brought every imaginable blessing into King Solomon's life, and into the lives of those around him.

Developing the ability to listen is a pursuit that has remained at the forefront of spirituality and personal development since the times of Solomon. Simply remembering what people tell us can be very difficult for human beings.[7] Why is it so hard? Our brains are able to process information much more quickly than the rate of human speech. That gap frees up the mind of a listener to wander.[8]

One technique to improve our listening skills is to focus on simply remembering what it is that we are hearing. Not only can this increase our likelihood of recalling a conversation, but it also activates the more empathetic parts of our brains, stimulates a feelings-based experience,[9] and brings us one step closer to walking in someone else's shoes.

Listening with the goal of evaluating, objecting, or responding to someone else uses a 'top-down' cognitive, analytical process, making it difficult to feel empathy and connection.

On the other hand, the act of asking and then listening draws out the natural passion in people, creating connection that registers in the brain as a form of pleasure.[10] We are, indeed, surrounded by people who know things that we may not. The act of listening affirms our belief that every person has a story, and a unique and valuable perspective to share.

Grow Your Insight # 5

Choose a conversation in which to intentionally omit the word 'I.' What will transpire? Reflect.

Insight #6: Listening to Ourselves to Connect

When was the last time you spoke to yourself aloud? Listening to our own authentic voice connects us with our depths. In order to tune in to our inner voice, we need to provide it the space in which to speak and be heard. Humans have countless thoughts per day, which may repeat over time whether or not we believe that they are true. However, we are not our thoughts. Our thoughts need not define us.

Is it possible to change an inner dialogue? In ancient Hebrew, the word for "speech" (dee - bur) has the same root as the word for "thing" (da - var). We can concretize thoughts into words by writing them down or verbalizing them. This process can help us notice conflicting ideas wandering through our minds at the same moment, and in expressing them clearly and thinking about our thoughts as 'things,' we move into metacognition, which is the process of thinking about our thinking.

This type of contemplation can help us recognize the thoughts we agree with, and those that have no connection with who we are or what we truly believe. When we examine a thought, we can ask ourselves, "Can this thought be substantiated with evidence? Is it possible that the opposite of this thought may also be partially or completely true?"

In quieting the noise of the outside world and providing ourselves with a personal platform to tune in to our thoughts and feelings, we are getting in touch with an inner voice and uniting with our own depths.

Grow Your Insight # 6

Take a few minutes and write down the thoughts that flow through your mind. Do not judge or qualify them. Simply write.

Read your list.

Which thoughts do you believe to be true?

Which can be substantiated with evidence?

Insight #7: Empathizing to Connect

Listening has the potential to take us out of our own minds and transport us into the minds and hearts of others. Quieting our own thoughts creates space for meaningful connections and attunes us to the subjective experiences of others.

How we experience life from our unique vantage points is subjective. The way we perceive what is happening, how we feel and think about that experience, is subject to the way we interpret it.

What we believe about how someone else is feeling may not be accurate. When we practice non-judgmental listening — listening to remember and understand, we obtain insight into the experience of others.

The next step in connecting is empathizing. Empathy helps us look for a genuine point of connection. When we observe the people around us, their experiences may appear unfamiliar or impossible to relate to. Perhaps we have never been through something similar, or we may consciously or subconsciously evaluate a decision as one we would not have made in their situation.

When we pay attention, we begin to notice the emotional tone of a conversation and gain insight. We can identify the feeling beneath the words we are hearing. In a conversation, we might ask, "How do you feel about this?" If we are honest with ourselves, we may have experienced a similar feeling.

Rather than approaching our experience of connection from the vantage point of a hero or a helper to someone we're unable to understand, through emotions, we can connect empathetically and see eye-to-eye. This is the language of the heart.

Grow Your Insight # 7

The next time you are in a conversation, listen closely and pay attention to the emotional experience of the speaker.

How does this create a sense of connection? Reflect.

Two

Awareness and Gratitude

"Miracles are all around us."
—Ruchoma Shain

Jerusalem, 2003, continued...

I raced out of the library and walked briskly to my destination.

Minutes later, I arrived. After ascending quickly up several flights of stairs, I was nearly breathless, face to face with a metal door standing between me and powerful yet peaceful energy beckoning my entrance.

"Come right in," a soft voice called from inside.

Captivated, and ready to help, I walked into a modest apartment. Books spanned the living room like wallpaper, their golden spines glimmering in the morning sunlight pouring through a large balcony window.

In front of the window, surrounded by the warm light, a small, gentle-looking older woman sat still on a fabric armchair.

She greeted me softly inviting me to sit down.

"Thank you for coming so quickly. It won't be long until my children arrive. If you could just help me to stand up?"

I reached out my hands to meet hers. She clasped on to me and lifted herself from the chair.

"Let's come into the kitchen and warm up a kettle for tea."

Slowly, we moved together to a small table just a few steps away. She gestured with her eyes toward a tea kettle sitting atop the stove.

She gazed at me with soft eyes and a sweet smile. "What brings you all the way here?"

"I... I'm..." I began, realizing that I hadn't entirely explained my reasons for this trip to anyone until now.

Something about being in this woman's presence brought words into my mouth. Here was an elderly woman, who despite her physical pain, took the time to listen to me. Someone she had never met, a fraction of her age, from across the world both physically and spiritually, and yet she made every effort to listen. And in her listening, I felt wholehearted that she truly cared about me.

"I'm looking for something. I'm not sure what… but I know that there is more to life than what I can see. Or touch."

She nodded, probing for more.

I told her about my high school side-job in the psychic bookstore, about my love affair with the sand and the sea and how magical it was to spend countless days at the shore during my childhood. I even told her about my friend in college, who was an atheist and inspired me to question everything I thought I knew about the world of spirituality.

I told her how I felt like I was searching for some purpose, meaning, or way to make sense of life, and to make the most of it all. She listened intently as her smile broadened and her eyebrows lifted in interest. "Miracles," she explained, "are all around us."

"I… I can't believe you're telling me about miracles. You'll never believe what happened to me this morning!"

She smiled, knowingly, and the kettle began to whistle on the stovetop.

I prepared two hot teas and returned to the table. "I'll tell you what," she continued. "We may appear to be speaking on a telephone by way of technology that connects us to people all over the world," she began, pointing to a light tan plastic telephone on the table. "We can also recognize that this very technology is miraculous."

I felt tears welling up in my eyes. Truth can be so simple and yet so profound all in the same breath.

"When we wake up in the morning and we can see, hear, think, and… live… this too is a great miracle. As you open your eyes to recognize and acknowledge all of the miracles in your life, the more that they will appear. You will have unlocked the gate to living with purpose."

One moment can create indelible impressions upon our souls. Those moments are pearls of wisdom to treasure, for their power to transform our lives.

This chapter presents insights about everyday living. The good fortune of living in a time of material abundance and convenience can obscure the joy and presence once gained from the art of living and engaging in physical work. Yet, it is always possible to reconnect with purpose, joy, and presence. Even one small act thought, or word may be enough to inspire that shift.

Insight #8: Tasks Versus Experiences

We can view our path in life as a sequence of tasks, or a sequence of experiences. When life is viewed as a list of tasks — tasks will be checked off, only to be replaced by others.

In slowing down, we can increase our presence within a moment. As we accomplish and achieve, we can remain mindful of the importance, depth, and purpose of our act, allowing ourselves to fully experience a moment.

We can envision the possible outcome an act, even one that may feel mundane. When laundering a shirt, we can visualize the person who will wear this shirt, and what our act enables them to do. What will be the ripple effect of our act?

I'll always remember my great-grandmother's washing board that hung on the garage wall in my childhood home. Just one hundred years ago, the act of laundering clothes was far more encompassing than it is today. Our ancestors drew water from a well, and were far more physically engaged in the acts of daily living. We can acknowledge the modern conveniences that we have while still remaining mindful of the value of a task at hand.

In slowing down and focusing on an act as an experience with far reaching value, we can tune in to the interconnectivity present even in daily tasks.

Grow Your Insight # 8

Reflect upon one task from your day. What was it?

What are the ripple effects of this task?

Insight #9: New Paradigms

Now that we have contemplated the ripple effect of our daily acts, we can begin to re-envision those acts as experiences worthy of enjoyment. Although we may not be predisposed toward a joyful presence, we can heed the call of our souls and feel uplifted in any moment.

Every moment is a gift. Some moments just need a bit more unwrapping than others. Even if a day appears to be ordinary, there may be a way to squeeze some joy out of it.

A great master of Torah, 'Rebbe Nachman of Breslov' lived in late eighteenth-century Eastern Europe. His community faced the challenges of daily living and harsh persecution. Rebbe Nachman taught that it is an obligation to live with joy. He explained that by nature, we are drawn to sadness. Yet, we can seek opportunities to infuse our lives with joy, and even playfulness.[1]

I may feel joy at the birth of a newborn baby, or grief and loss when faced with tragedy. Within the human experience, it is a normal part of our overall well-being to experience a range of emotions such as these. Yet, when it comes to our daily living, we can embrace the idea that if we need to do something, we have every reason to try and enjoy it. Rather than believing, "I'll be happy at a future point in time when something changes or something is accomplished," we can believe that happiness is possible in the here and now.

We cannot underestimate the influence of other people in our lives, and in fact, human emotions can be contagious.[2] We make choices about who to surround ourselves with. Attaching ourselves to honest people who strive for goodness and optimism can transform our lives.

As we endeavor to live with more joy, honesty, and empathy, we are influencing those around us. We may begin to tap into these same traits in others that we could not see before.

As we develop the habit of seeking advice from others, we become happiness researchers. When we observe people undertaking certain tasks and seemingly enjoying them, we can ask them about their processes.

Laundry has not always been my favorite task. Envisioning piles and piles of washing and folding clothing for the six people in our family, I did not always relish the prospects. In the same breath, I knew this was a first-world problem, and I did not want to invest mental energy allowing negativity to consume me.

One day, while visiting a friend, I noticed my friend's laundry room.

I glanced inside and immediately noticed her neatly folded, freshly washed and dried stacks of laundry gracing six separate baskets. She had a large family, lots of laundry, and she had somehow made it all look nice and neat. I would even call it pretty. I marveled out loud at her work.

"Did you seriously fold all of this laundry?" I asked her, in shock.

"Laundry is Zen," she responded.

"Zen?" I pushed her a bit further.

"Folding and organizing relaxes me," she answered. And with that simple answer, my paradigm shifted. I pondered the act of folding, considering its similarity to creating intricate and beautiful paper origami objects.

I realized that with a sense of focus and precision, I could organize the physical clothing in my home to look nice, neat, and even radiant for my family to use and enjoy. It only took one moment and one reframe to relate differently to this act and begin to enjoy it.

If there are tasks we need to do, why not attempt to enjoy them in the process? If we accept the reality of the present moment, we can reframe the way that we experience it. If I must do laundry, how can I enjoy it? I can think differently about the process (laundry is Zen), and I can approach the task with a new methodology (focusing on precision in folding and making the clothing look beautiful).

Some people may find a sense of meaning and purpose in outsourcing certain tasks to focus on other projects, work, or interests. While the decision of what to outsource and to whom is all yours, I believe that we can seek new paradigms for the work in life we choose to or need to complete on our own.

Everyday creative acts can be uplifting for our moods.[3] Re-imagining our tasks and finding new paradigms opens up the possibility for greater levels of enjoyment. This world is full of people who love all sorts of things and find ways of making even seemingly mundane tasks more joyful and meaningful.

Grow Your Insight # 9

Have you ever experienced a shift in your perspective that has brought meaning and enjoyment into your daily routine?

What was it? How did it change your outlook?

Focus on one component of your routine that could benefit from a paradigm shift. What would that shift look like, and how could it bring more joy into your life?

Insight # 10: Awaken in Gratitude

Expressing gratitude increases the feeling of happiness.[4] While the science of gratitude is new, the practice of expressing gratitude is not. "Grateful" is the first word on my lips each morning, because it is part of an ancient Torah spiritual practice dating back thousands of years.[5]

The ancient recitation is: "Grateful am I before you, Ruler of all living existence, That has returned my soul. How great is Your faith."

Within this recitation, "grateful" appears before the word "I," reminding me each morning to focus on what I'm grateful for before I shift my focus toward anything else. This one act upon awakening creates an asset orientation in the mind, turning the attention to what *is* rather than what *is not*. We are setting ourselves up to shift away from focusing on deficits – what we appear to lack - and toward noticing the assets in our lives.

In order to counter our thoughts of sadness and worry, we can seek to live a life of service. The most interesting and meaningful aspect of our lives is that which we are able to do for others.[6]

When we wake up each morning, we can focus our attention on what we have been given so that we can make this world better! One smile, one gesture, or one act of kindness changes the world for eternity.

Grow Your Insight # 10

When you awaken, recite a gratitude mantra.
"Grateful am I."

What are you grateful for in this moment?

Insight # 11: Anchoring with Stillness

L ife is like an ocean. We observe it's choppy surface, changing by the moment, unpredictably. And then as we dip our toes inside, lowering ourselves further, we descend into continually calmer waters, the deeper we descend. Here, in the deepest depths of the ocean lies serenity. Here, there is always still and calm.

As we move through life, we face appearances and impressions. We move through our day, engage with our surroundings, and emotions may rise and fall like waves on the surface. Beneath the surface of these emotions and thoughts swirling through the mind, at all times there is a place of stillness and calm that has always been there and will always be there. Awareness of this place anchors our being in stillness.

If we yell and scream at the waves, they will not subside.

Floating on the surface of the ocean, one must protect itself from the harsh elements. The mind lives on the surface. It may jump to conclusions to protect the pure and gentle soul. It can not risk rejection.

What happens when we connect to the deeper parts of ourselves? We are always safe within the cocoon of Infinite waters. The heart lives in the depths.

Grow Your Insight # 11

Consider a moment when you feel stressed, worried, or anxious. Connect with your breath and envision yourself being transported down beneath the choppy surface of the ocean, into the depths, where all is calm and still. Anchor yourself with stillness by simply focusing upon your breath and envisioning yourself in this place of calm and stillness.

Insight # 12: Expressing Gratitude

People will go to the ends of the earth for us when they feel appreciated. How can we express thanks to others and invite them into our lives? Presence in the lives of one another is one of life's greatest gifts.

We can create events and celebrations and invite guests. We can celebrate birthdays or honor the departed. We can gather to give thanks for our health or new milestones in life. I'll always remember being invited to a meal of thanks for one of my teachers after she survived a life-threatening situation. Hearing her story as she shared with friends and community was deeply touching and inspiring.

Opening our homes can be a spiritual act and an act of gratitude. At the end of his life, King David offered his son words of wisdom about how to express appreciation. He instructed his son Solomon to offer kindness to those that have shown him favor, and to always offer them a place at his table.[7] Creating and sustaining friendships can improve our health and lengthen our lives.[8] Opening our homes is opening our hearts.

Grow Your Insight # 12

How could you express gratitude by inviting people into your home or to a gathering?

Who would you like to connect with?

Insight # 13: Saying 'Thank You'

When was the last time you wrote a paper 'thank-you' note? Today's technology normalized the abbreviating our thank-yous into a 'tysm' 'thx,' a 'ty,' or even an emoji.

We now know that most people underestimate the positive impact of their expressions of gratitude, mistakenly believing that the recipient of thanks already knows of their appreciation.[9]

In written thank-you's, people generally tend toward being concerned if they are getting the words 'just right.' Knowing the degree of delight that letter recipients actually have, and of how little the wording really matters, we could be more inclined to write thank-you notes.

Recently, I investigated this research in my own life. Admittedly, I've been tech-centric in my thank-you-ing practices, and so I thought this exercise of note-writing could be enlightening. I immediately thought of two friends who had recently done something nice for me. I wrote a note one for each friend – to be hand-delivered. Each note expressed appreciation for the friend's kindness and friendship.

To my surprise, each of the recipients were teary eyed when reading these seemingly simple notes. This is the power of a small change to make a big difference.

Grow Your Insight # 13

Hand write a thank-you note to someone who you're grateful for.

Insight # 14: Absence and Presence

The traditional morning gratitude recitation makes a reference to our soul having been returned to our bodies upon our awakening. Beyond our souls being returned to us, we can also consider that waking up alive is a privilege and not an absolute.

The initial reaction to thinking about death may be one of fear. And yet, many of those who are faced with death and survive often transform and turn over a new leaf in life, able to live more authentically and joyfully.

The practice of contemplating one's own death is correlated with thinking more positively after the contemplation.[10] Sometimes, it is in considering an absence that we learn to appreciate a presence. We find a thought-provoking and inspiring idea about exactly this, written by the sagely "Aish Kodesh" in the early twentieth century:

"Everyone has a G-dly level of consciousness within. It's just that one's desires … conceal and obscure it... Since a person is constantly running after his desires... his thoughts continue to flood him without end. One should, therefore, imagine in his mind, that he, Heaven forbid, has no tomorrow. He will then not be forced to think about his tomorrow, and he won't continue to be disturbed and distracted by his desires."[11]

Grow Your Insight # 14

Contemplate life without something — anything —
that you are accustomed to. Reflect.

Three

How to See the Forest

"Everything is a gift."

Night fell upon the city, and I felt a sense of serenity sweeping over me as I wove my way down side streets and alleyways toward home. My day had been something out of a storybook, and I hung in suspense for what might unfold next. And yet, there was an energy from my miraculous encounter that put me at ease.

Walking past the open market and swaths of bold, bright-colored fabrics and gold glittering sequined scarves framed my view. I felt I had been placed on a spiritual path, and it felt more vibrant than I had ever imagined.

I arrived home to our sparsely furnished one-bedroom unit with a kitchen window overlooking a forested park. Our visitors marveled at the forest view, and at the minimalistic way in which we were living.

After arriving from California, we had purchased everything that we needed for the year stretched out before us: two ceramic plates, two sets of cutlery, one pan, two drinking glasses, and two tea cups. We brought one suitcase of clothing each, and that was what we lived with during that year.

I made my way into the kitchen to prepare dinner.

For a moment, my thoughts drifted across the world to California, where I was raised, where we had been married, and where we had first decided to take this journey together.

I felt gratitude for my beloved family and friends back home. There were moments where I missed the comforts of life there, like the soft carpeting which had been squarely replaced in Jerusalem by the low maintenance hard stone floors.

In spite of what I missed, I knew that each stone step was leading me through an ancient land, rife with deep and spiritual teachings. I felt inspired to live simply and to continue learning.

I had established my own, unique and personal relationship with the Infinite. And this was a bliss second to none.

The insights in this chapter introduce the idea that there can be seeds of rebirth sown into what appears as destruction. The good in life may be hiding in plain sight, and when we search for and notice it, we become aware of the interconnectedness of parts comprising a whole.

Insight # 15: The Glimmer of Hope

Noticing "coincidences" can attune us to the possibility of a bigger picture of life.

The Infinite Being that created and sustains this world has a miraculous way of orchestrating this universe.

Recently, I heard a story of a nearby community here in Israel that experienced near complete devastation after almost all of its homes were burned down by arson. This one small community of a few thousand people lost homes, possessions, work and family media on hard drives and everything else that had graced their homes. Absolute devastation and loss ensued after this fire.

And yet, as spiritual seekers, some found hidden blessings in this time of devastation. One woman who, just the day before the fire, received all of the medications necessary to begin a course of fertility treatments. She and her husband had been trying unsuccessfully to have children for years.

After the fire, the couple returned to their home and found the treatments destroyed. This was a significant financial loss, but the couple began saving up for more treatments immediately.

Just two months later, they discovered that they had been expecting a child since before their home was destroyed. This meant that if the treatments had not been destroyed in the fire, they could have caused life-threatening harm to what had been at the time a brand-new life, beginning to grow.

Stories such as these which remind us we may not always understand the big picture or the blessings that may be hidden in our challenges. We may find that even within the aftermath of destruction, seeds of hope have been sown.

Grow Your Insight # 15

Do you notice sparks of good or hidden gifts in your memories of challenges? What have you learned and integrated into yourself after having moved through challenging experiences?

Insight # 16: What we Notice

It is quite possible to live through a miracle and simply not recognize it. So much of life is not about what happens to us, or how we respond, but what we notice in the process.

Humans have a tendency toward viewing life pessimistically. This phenomenon is known as "the negativity bias." Essentially, this means that if we hear a variety of ideas about someone or something, it will be the negative ones that make the strongest impression upon us.[1]

When we look at a mosaic with hundreds of pieces, our eye may be drawn, almost magically, to the one missing. A tendency to focus on the negative can occupy the mind in other ways. People spend more time looking at sad or scary pictures than they do looking at beautiful ones.

Similarly, a phenomenon called 'loss aversion' explains that human beings are more averse to losing money than they are excited about being gifted the same amount.[2] In the mind, a loss feels more potent than a gain. This is one reason people may appear to lead relatively healthy, productive, and outwardly successful lives and all the while suffer tremendously on a psychological level.

How can we transcend the predisposition toward negativity? Learning to focus on the good is a skill acquired through practice.

Torah wisdom teaches us that true wealth is happiness with our lot.[3] This does not idealize complacency with what we have. While we can strive to achieve or attain more, we will only taste the sweetness of our victories and attainments when we train ourselves to notice and appreciate the good in our present situation.

Negativity, in itself, may contain positivity. The negativity bias and phenomenon of loss aversion have benefited human survival. We are wired to live, innovate, and create. We notice what is broken to fix it. We realize sadness in someone and offer them comfort or consolation. We see pain and offer compassion or healing. In these situations, our awareness of what is missing is positive in its ability to inspire us to act.

In the world of our thoughts, we remain free to choose where we will place our focus. One good thought has more power than we can even imagine.

If a thought or mindset is not productive or assistive in furthering us along our path of truth, we can thank it for its service and bid it farewell. In thinking about our thinking, we adjust our thoughts to align with our authentic selves.

Grow Your Insight # 16

Reflect upon a negative thought or idea which may be revisiting your mind regularly. How has that thought served you or protected you in the past?

Why is it not serving or helping you today?

Where will you be without that thought?

Insight # 17: True Wealth

If being happy with what we have right now is the key to having true wealth, how do we grow our appreciation and enjoyment in the present moment?

Once, a young child told her teacher that she wanted to be rich. The teacher asked: "why?"

"I will be happy," the child whispered innocently.

"I can make you rich, but first, I must ask: Will you give me your hand if I pay you all of the money in the world?" The teacher inquired.

"I will not give you my hand," she answered with certainty.

"It appears that you are already very rich," the teacher affirmed.

Just like this young child, we can shift our awareness to notice what we already have. Chances are, there is nothing you would trade for so much of what is already right in your life at this exact moment.

Contemplating life without something that we are accustomed to having can bring us a sense of appreciation. Something broken, missing, or lost may be enough at times to foster a newfound sense of appreciation for what we have.

We can, in any moment, contemplate the gifts and abilities which we are afforded through that which already exists in our life.

As we develop and express our gratitude, we attune our eyes, our ears, our minds, and our hearts to notice there is always more goodness and kindness in this world than there is of anything else.

Grow Your Insight # 17

Contemplate one thing in your life at this moment which is helping you. Consider the myriad ways in which it enriches your life. Reflect.

Insight #18: Awe and Humility

There are over seven billion people on planet Earth, and yet, in many places, human beings have never felt more alone.[4] We strive to successfully navigate relationships and foster close human connections, and yet it is not done easily. Social connectedness naturally improves health and extends lives.

You are uniquely qualified with everything that you need to cultivate close and meaningful relationships. What is your most valuable asset in creating and sustaining those relationships?

Moses, the leader of the ancient Israelites, was a masterful leader and beloved by his people. He was permitted a partial viewing of the Infinite and was left glowing with a light so radiant that it was blinding to anyone who gazed at him. One might imagine that he walked away from this moment full of pride or with a sense of privilege. Yet, Moses is noted for his humility. It was this trait which enabled him to connect with people and succeed in his position of influence and leadership.

When exposed to awe-inspiring sights and experiences, we are humbled. One recent study of humility divided participants into two groups and placed them in rooms to watch videos.[5] Half watched videos specifically intended to inspire awe, and the other group watched something else. Next, they were asked to rate their personal strengths and weaknesses.

After watching the awe-inspiring videos, participants made self-assessments in a 'more balanced way,' acknowledging the role of luck, other people, or a 'Greater Being' in their strengths and achievements. Those who did not watch the awe-inspiring videos were more likely to take personal credit.

How can we fill our lives with awe and wonder? We can step out and immerse ourselves in breathtaking nature or visit far-flung places that differ from our usual surroundings. Simply visualizing an awe-inspiring sight in nature can transport us to that scene and evoke feelings of both awe and humility.

At any moment, we can slow down and notice the intricate beauty of one delicate flower, or even the unique pattern inside of our own hands. We can delve into the mysteries of science, inspiring historical legends, or even the seemingly ordinary lives of the people around us. Awe is hiding in plain sight.

Grow Your Insight # 18

Recall a moment of awe. Where were you? What were the sights, sounds, and sensations at this time?

Pause, and immerse yourself in the vision of that awe. Reflect.

Insight # 19: Behind the Veil

F eelings of awe can be inspired by experiences out and about in the great wide world of sweeping views and far-off treks. At the same time, it is also possible to inspire our sense of awe without leaving home.

The complete production line for nearly anything in our lives can expand exponentially as we trace its origin. How many people have contributed to what's on your dinner plate? Even locally grown produce involves a vast number of people, and all the more so those items in our lives which have gone through the global supply chain.

To inspire a bit of awe and gratitude into our minds and hearts, we can attempt to trace the history of something in our possession. Who is hiding behind the veil of this moment?

Grow Your Insight # 19

Contemplate the origins of one item in your possession. Who or what has been a part of process in joining you?

Insight # 20: Noticing Goodness

An ancient poem begins by asking, "A woman of valor, who can find?" It outlines the traits of a wonderful woman, and then at the end, proclaims, "There are many great women... but you outshine them all!"

How is it this poem begins by searching for a good woman, and then ends by proclaiming there are many? This reveals a secret to finding the good in people, and finding the good in our surroundings.

By way of acknowledging the good that we see in everyone and everything that surrounds us, we begin to realize how much greatness is concealed behind the veil.

How can we accustom ourselves to notice and nurture the good in ourselves and in others? One practice is to begin mindfully and honestly complimenting that which we appreciate.

We can apply this practice in our personal relationships. Sharing positive feedback has also proven to be an effective practice in the professional sphere in its ability to bring out the highest levels of productivity and creativity in work.[6]

Most people in our lives will not benefit from a critique unless they are asking us for feedback. Chances are, they give themselves more than enough criticism. We can opt to offer helpful suggestions or ideas, being sensitive to when, how, and if our insights will be received. Most powerfully, we can focus on and acknowledge that which we love, admire, and appreciate. See the good and watch it blossom.

Grow Your Insight # 20

Picture a loved one or a friend. What do you appreciate about this person? Reflect.

What do you appreciate about yourself, or what are you proud of? Reflect.

Insight #21: What Makes Love Real

How many songs, poems, and works of art have been composed about love? We are uniquely designed to give and receive love.

I'll always remember grandparents of blessed memory as pillars of love and exemplars of commitment. Once, as a young child, I sat in their kitchen and observed a moment which engraved itself into my consciousness.

It was evening, and the glow of sunset illuminated the courtyard on the other side of the kitchen window. I watched as my grandfather was arriving home from work, briefcase in hand, walking toward the door. He was whistling, as usual, but something was different about his gaze. I sat and observed as my grandmother greeted him at the door with a warm smile.

As it had happened, my grandfather's eyes were troubling him that afternoon. Without hesitating, my grandmother knew exactly what he needed and gently dispensed eye drops into his eyes.

Watching my strong and dignified grandparents in this moment was curiously endearing to me. "Grandma?" my younger self began, uncertain what I would be asking yet knowing there was a question waiting for its answer.

She sensed my question before I asked and opened her mouth in wisdom: "I'll tell you what I've learned about love and commitment. Love is not only the good times. Love can be good, and sometimes it is easy to love. But what makes love real is when a challenge arises and you remain committed."

In the Hebrew language, the word for love is "Ahava." Its root word means "give, care for, or nurture." The very word for love in Hebrew instructs us that love is more than just a 'feeling,' and how in its purest form, it is an ongoing act of giving.

In its wisdom, the Hebrew language includes a numerical value for each letter in the alphabet. The word "Ahava" includes an *aleph* (value of 1), *hey* (value of five), *bet* (value of two), and *hey* (another value of five). When added up, these numbers total thirteen.

An interesting connection, the word for the number "one" in Hebrew is "echad." It's numerical value (*aleph* - 1, *khet* - 8, *daled* - 4) also equals thirteen. It is our love that enables us to transcend selfishness and experience the feeling oneness and unity.

Grow Your Insight # 21

Picture a loved one or a friend important to you. How does this person appreciate being given to?

What do you enjoy receiving from a loved one or friend? How can you communicate

Four

How to Be Kind

"To be kind is more important than to be right. Many times, what people need is not a brilliant mind that speaks, but a special heart that listens."
-Rabbi Menachem Mendel Schneerson,
The Seventh Rebbe of Lubavitch

When we live our lives from a place of noticing the miraculous, we come from a place of awe and humility. Realizing the wonder in the universe leads us to the understanding that we are also wondrous creatures. This chapter is about connecting to the love within us and reflecting that love into the universe.

Insight # 22: Our Love is a Mirror

A young child, feeling wounded, seeks help from her teacher to mediate her social world. In seeking help, she is saying, 'I do not know how to protect myself from the feelings, the words, the actions of those around me.'

This child, relying on another, will carry forth her victimhood until the day that she learns to love herself fully. The wounds of her past have been buried so deeply within her, that with the slightest shaking of her tree, she is pierced to the core. How will she learn to love herself enough in order to heal?

"Shhhhhhhhh....." the teacher whispers.

In this silence, the young child hears the stirring of her soul. Within her, a peace, which she buried so deeply awakens her knowing. Yes, it is safe to love. For it is only the love which sprouts from within that grows into shelter ... a canopy of shade in which peace can blossom. She basks in the shade of this peace, knowing in all moments that only the loving ones will enter.

In the order of ancient morning Torah blessings, it reads: 'I hereby take on the commandment of loving my fellow as I love myself.'[1] What does it mean to love another as yourself?

Love is the primary vessel through which peace is created. Loving another and creating peace can only begin with self-love. Contemplate the way that you speak to yourself, think to yourself, and care for yourself, and you will find a mirror for the way in which you are relating to others.

Grow Your Insight # 22

Visualize stepping outside of your own body for a moment, and picture yourself as a child. Give yourself words of appreciation and encouragement.

Insight # 23: The Shelter of Peace

We have awakened to the possibility that we can love ourselves more. Realization is the birth of possibility. Where do we go from here?

Begin in your physical home, the body you are living in, for as it has been said by the great sage and doctor Rambam, "Maintaining a healthy and sound body is among the ways of servicing the Infinite, for one cannot understand or have any knowledge of the Infinite if one is ill." [2]

Nearly one thousand years later, neuroscience and integrative medicine agree that both food and movement play a crucial role in our overall picture of health.[3 4] As Eastern healing and Western medicine are meeting, we are clarifying the synergy of spiritual and physical well-being once and for all.

While an inundation of information and clever marketing compete for our attention and devotion to particular modalities of wellness, we can remember simply that our physical vessels are sacred and must be honored accordingly.

Our bodies have been created and are being sustained by The Infinite. Our surroundings, both people and resources, are the vessels and Divine messengers through which we can receive healing. In acknowledging physical care as Divine Service, you are partnering with the Infinite and aligning your body, mind, and soul with the Source of all Health.

While I may trust in a doctor or healer to administer the best care known to their field of practice, I know that miracles of healing have taken place, even for some who, according to science, were deemed hopeless. When we acknowledge our True Healer, working through the hands of human practitioners, nothing is outside of the realm of possibility. There is always hope.

Grow Your Insight # 23

How do you prioritize your physical care?
What would an upgrade look like for you?

Reflect.

Insight # 24: Falling into Possibility

So much life is spent either seeking love, aiming to maintain a love relationship, or recovering from the loss of a loved one. Popular fiction in movies and romance novels have taught us that love is 'fallen into.' Can we actually 'fall' in love?

In the Torah, episodes of 'falling in love' seem to occur from the first moment of creation. Adam expresses emotional excitement at the appearance of Eve. Rebecca sees Isaac and almost falls off her camel, knowing she will be betrothed to him. Jacob's attraction to Rachel empowers him to lift an exceptionally heavy boulder he would not ordinarily be capable of lifting. There is and always has been great power in romantic attraction.

In recent years, 'love at first sight' also appears to be a common phenomenon. As it has been studied — for those believing in the concept, there is a 60% chance it will happen.[5]

What is romantic attraction based upon, and what attracts people to one another? Functional magnetic resonance imaging (fMRI) studies have looked at the brain in its state of romantic attraction and identified twelve areas of the brain working in conjunction to simultaneously produce specific feelings experienced as 'falling in love.' The state of falling in love can be differentiated from a state of mere attraction, using this brain imaging technology to locate activation in different regions of the brain during these two experiences.[6]

In its complexity, part of the emotional state of being in love includes habit formation and having repeated, shared emotional experiences with another person and contributing to the relationship. Passionate love is both a basic and a complex brain process — while it shares certain features with feelings of physical attraction, what differentiates love from mere attraction is the intense desire to be united with one person to the exclusion of anyone else.

Love is enduring, and science is discovering that the feelings of falling in love can be sustained when people are actively working on relationships and investing in the goals of the partnership.[7] Brain imaging studies looking at the neural activity of couples married for over twenty years confirm that the feeling of love can withstand the test of time. Benefits of maintaining a love relationship include feelings of reduced stress and greater happiness. These relationships are built when couples make an effort on behalf of one another.

An interesting parallel, Torah wisdom maintains that marriage is not the meeting of two individuals, but rather, it is the reunification of one complete soul.

Grow Your Insight # 24

Do you believe in 'falling in love'? What are the characteristics or qualities that would inspire you (or do inspire you) to be united with another person?

Insight # 25: Loving is Knowing, Loving is Giving

In the Torah, love is presented as a type of 'knowledge,' as in an intimate cognitive knowing, and a physical knowing. We first see this word in Genesis 4:1 when Adam 'knew' his wife, Eve.

Is seeking to love and be loved even a possibility if we do not have an awareness of ourselves? An essential component in any relationship is giving; giving of time, energy, and resources. Giving of our authentic ideas and opinions. Giving of our attention and affection. Is it possible to give authentically if we cannot hear our inner voice and do not know what it is that are authentically able to give?

With self-awareness and knowledge of our authentic makeup, we come to learn what it is that we have to give. There are two ways of viewing relationships. With a 'fixed' perspective, one believes that compatibility equals an effortless relationship.

With a 'growth-oriented' perspective, one realizes that ongoing effort is the main ingredient in a sustainable type of love. In knowing ourselves, we know what it is that we are able to give. In knowing another, we come to learn what it is that they need.

Seeking love without self-knowledge is like grasping for water with an open hand and trying to hold on to it. Everything slips through the cracks.

Loving from a place of wholeness, self-knowledge and acceptance, is an eternal dance of sharing life's beauty. The palm is closed, girded in strength, and almost magically, it becomes a vessel carrying water.

Grow Your Insight # 25

When you take action on behalf of a loved one,
notice the far-reaching effects of your act.
How do your actions affect your loved one?

Insight #26: The Love for a Baby

A mother becomes a mother with the birth of her first child. She feels a love unlike any other. It is a perfect love, which seeks to give the purest goodness and kindness conceivable.

She marvels at a feeling of wholeness in caring for her tiny, newly born baby. So small and so helpless is this infant, and yet, he is the source of a perfect love.

She could not have imagined a love so perfect before it came into being.

She asks, "how will it be possible to love another with such wholeness, and without taking away from this perfect love?"

Her heart knows no bounds. Another perfect love blossoms, watered with compassion, like the offshoot of a tree … growing… flourishing into its own.

How is it possible that this is so carefully shading, watering, and nurturing a tiny seedling that one can feel such blissful perfection?

She is needed to nurture life, and she knows, so deeply, that this is the greatest of all gifts.

The Infinite one has created us and continues to sustain us in all moments. Our capacity to breathe, and do anything in this world is reliant upon factors outside of our own control.

The Infinite is nurturing us because we are needed by It. We have been created and sustained by It. This can only be for a purpose.

In our giving and in our nurturing, we embody the Infinite. This is the deepest and purest of all joys.

In Hebrew, the word for 'give' is 'natan,' spelled nun - tav - nun. It is spelled the same in both directions, a symbol for the act of giving.

To give is to receive, and to receive is to give.

Grow Your Insight # 26

Where can we give of ourselves in life to love and appreciate someone even more?

Insight # 27 : A Good Eye

Once, a young boy set out on a journey to understand the world. He began by asking his teacher, "Why have we been created with two eyes?"

His teacher responded: "With the left eye, look at yourself, and see where you need to improve. With the right eye, look at others, seeking out their best qualities."

As we use the left eye to look inward, we can accept ourselves, forgive ourselves, and reflect upon the past in order to visualize evolution and growth.

Look inside yourself and notice a seed. You have been given this seed, a one-of-a-kind. Only you have the tools and resources to nurture its growth. As you see the good surrounding and supporting you, your seed begins to sprout, open, and blossom. It is watered with compassion and absorbing the light of truth, it radiates its beauty throughout your being, awakening the senses to notice all that is no longer concealed. Your seed has been placed within you to grow. As you nurture your seed, you nurture your soul.

Grow Your Insight # 27

What is an act of goodness that you have seen, and how does it inspire you to act?

How have you been supported or nurtured by an act of kindness?

Insight # 28: A Good Heart

In ancient times, the question was posed to the sages: "what is the greatest of all character traits in life?"

One after the other, the sages answered: "having a good eye, being a good friend, being a good neighbor, being considerate of consequences, having a good heart."

As it is explained, a good heart is the ultimate character trait, because it encompasses all of the others.[8] What does it mean to have a good heart? Having a good heart includes having a good eye; training ourselves to notice the good and the light, even in dark times. It is being a good friend by sharing in the joy of others, celebrating their successes, and being present in times of need. It is being a good neighbor by allowing ourselves not to be jealous or envious — and realizing that the blueprint of creation has allowed for billions of unique people in this world and there is room for all of us.

The sages understood human nature. They didn't hide or cover up our shortcomings or imperfections. They spoke without judgment. And on the journey of life, as we strive to outgrow instinctive reactions, we find joy in our self-development and self-expression.

This is what spirituality is all about. It's not about ignoring or denying nature or the world, but about living in it and with it to enrich our human experience.

Grow Your Insight # 28

How can you make yourself into a student of this world?
What does having a good heart look like for you?

Five

Existential Partnership

"It takes a village."

Contemplate for a moment the ways in which the notion of community has changed and shifted over the course of time. What was that old adage that it 'takes a village' in life to raise children? Where are we left in a day and age where most people are not living in villages, and when our co-existence no longer necessitates social interactions?

We have the potential to influence and inspire one another, and provide support and friendship which, in turn, has the power to enhance our health and extend our lives. People in our surroundings have the potential to become our partners in existence. This chapter is devoted to the ways in which we can cultivate community, harmony, collaboration, and existential partnership in our lives.

Insight # 29: Warmth in our Homes

Once, there was a young boy who grew up in a home full of beautiful objects. His parents loved their treasure collections so much it often seemed to the boy they valued their possessions more than their children. The young boy knew, deep in his heart, that people of any age were far more valuable than silver or even gold.

He felt called to leave the home of his parents. It was the only home he'd ever known, and it took great courage for him to go. He became a wanderer, a nomad, and a stranger in unknown lands.

He began to suffer from deep pangs of loneliness, and from the sense that he did not belong in a world which seemed to value its creations more than its creators.

As he journeyed, he spent nights under blankets of stars. He gazed into the natural world and realized that just as the stars had been created, so too had he. He alone had not created his feelings of loneliness or suffering.

As he wandered, he began discovering other wanderers, and he saw himself in their grim expressions of loneliness. He had experienced what he now knew to be a universal state of suffering.

And so he took his suffering, and the suffering he had witnessed in others and built himself a tent. He grew into a young man, found himself a wife, and together, they transformed a tent into a home.

It was not a home made of concrete walls. It was a tent which they opened, both literally and figuratively, as a refuge for lonely wanderers.

Rather than allowing loneliness and suffering to lead him into bitterness, the young man transformed his pain by creating a refuge of belonging. He understood the pain of being estranged and responded by living a life of radical hospitality.

In some parts of the world, people are well acquainted with their neighbors. While in our modern society, we have basically eradicated our 'need' to know our neighbors, we no longer rely on our neighbors for trading goods or services. Our modes of transport enable us to move far beyond the confines of our immediate surroundings within short spans of time.

So, in the western world, most urban dwellers are not acquainted with, or in frequent contact with the majority of their neighbors.[1] In days gone by, communities shared resources like ovens and water wells. The strength of such a community was in its members' abilities to divide and conquer daily tasks so that it could survive or even thrive. Relationships were a necessity.

Although that necessity for neighbors seems a bygone in many respects, according to longevity experts, a sense of community contributes to lengthening our lives and improving our health.[2] How can we begin to connect to those around us?

Connectivity begins with a pleasant face. A genuine smile, as the Torah has taught, nourishes its receiver like a glass of milk.[3] In fact, our nonverbal expressions influence the emotions of those around us. A real happiness expression is detectable both emotionally and visually. It is a smile which stretches up into the cheek muscles.[4] We are designed to sense the authenticity of expression.

One smile has tremendous power to spread joy and light in the world.

Grow Your Insight #29

What are some thoughts that bring
a genuine smile to your face?

Insight # 30: Feeling at Home in the World

Perhaps you have experienced hospitality in your surroundings. How do you know when you are welcome, and what do you observe in your surroundings that fosters this feeling?

Our family experienced what I call 'radical' hospitality when we immigrated to Israel. Our home was filled with goods from neighbors for days after our arrival. For months, we had weekly invitations for Friday evening dinners with one neighboring family or another.

Upon hearing about our warm welcome, my dear aunt, of blessed memory, shared with me about a tradition called the "welcome wagon," from her 1950's childhood in California. New neighbors were welcomed with meals and cards when they moved in. These acts of kindness had made an indelible and lifelong impression on her heart.

When I reflect back upon our experience being welcomed, one evening stands out distinctly in my memory. Our hosts greeted us warmly, served a delicious meal, expressed genuine interest in getting to know us, and when the evening eventually came to a close, they walked us home. While there is a traditional Torah practice of greeting guests at the door and walking them out, our hosts took it upon themselves to walk us several blocks to our door.

Escorting our guests in and out of our homes is a welcoming gesture and a beautiful way to create the feeling of a collective experience.

Grow Your Insight # 30

How can you incorporate the practice of escorting guests into your life?

Insight # 31: Social Trust

Whether we're welcoming guests into our homes, connecting with friends, or speaking with colleagues, we have the power to transmit words that build and inspire goodness in ourselves and in the world around us. Speaking is a form of spiritual practice, and it is believed by some that words in and of themselves have the power to create.

The famous expression uttered by a magician 'Abra C'Dabra' is derived from the Hebrew phrase "I will create as is the spoken word." Our words have a tremendous - bordering on magical - power to affect reality. This story illustrates this potential:

Once there was a man living in a small village who very much enjoyed gossiping. Working in business, he positioned himself as the center of attention, always full of exciting stories about other people. For years, he conducted his business affairs and gossiped to his heart's content, until one day, his reckless gossip victimized one too many, and his professional reputation tarnished. After years of success — being an entertainer at the expense of others — people stopped trusting him, and his business suffered.

Dealing with loss upon loss, the man grew hopeless. So, he turned to a wise sage, known as "Chafetz Chaim" which means "The One who Wills Life." The sage agreed to meet with the businessman, instructing him to bring one feather pillow. The two met and the sage led him up to the roof of his office building.

"I need your help," pleaded the businessman. I cannot stop speaking badly about other people, and it is now ruining my business.

"Here is a feather pillow," the sage replied. "Take it in your hands and rip it wide open with all of your might."

"We're on the roof!" the man retorted. "The feathers will go flying everywhere!" But the sage would not be persuaded.

And so, the man took the pillow, and with all of his might, tore it open and immediately, feathers went flying in every direction. Carried by gusts of winds over roofs and treetops, innumerable, tiny white feathers made their way into the distance.

"Very nice," the sage responded. "Now put them all back in."

The man was sorely dejected by the idea of gathering every single feather. A man of reason, he knew that this would be an impossible task.

"Ah...," answered the sage. "Just as with feathers, so too do words spread further than we can imagine. Once they are gone, they are gone forever."

Immediately, the man saw clearly that his words had far-reaching effects, and that popularity for gossiping was not popularity worth attaining.

What we hear about people affects our brains. One recent study examined the influence of gossip in our visual processing using a process called binocular rivalry.[5] Binocular rivalry presents one image to each eye, the two eyes compete for dominance, and then only one image appears. Participants were given information — positive, negative, or neutral, about a variety of faces. Then, the faces were presented visually. Repeatedly, the faces associated with negative information dominated the participants' focus, demonstrating that negative gossip influences the mind disproportionately.

Chances are that you don't need to learn about binocular rivalry to grasp this lesson. We can make the conscious choice to use our words to build and inspire, rather than succumbing to the temptation to speak mindlessly.

Grow Your Insight # 31

Do you find yourself tempted to gossip? Why do you think that maybe, and how could it be avoided?

Insight # 32: The Opposite of Good

O ne small change in our speech can make huge impacts on the quality of our relationships. Taking time to mindfully consider our intentions in sharing information can help us refine our words.

Imagine saying something positive about a political figure in the presence of a friend who supports an opposing political party. This could, easily enough, stir up conflict. In our times, people are coming to know this very well.

Understood more loosely, speaking in an overly positive manner about anyone could stir up resentment, jealousy, and negativity in even the most well-intentioned listener. As well-intentioned as anyone can be, there is a human tendency toward jealousy.

We can ask ourselves if what we are about to say, even if positive, has a constructive purpose. Why does your friend need to hear about someone else's success? Is what you are sharing intended to educate or share useful information, or merely to entertain or project yourself in a certain light?

Studies of 'positive 'gossip,' in the workplace have found that employees who speak more about colleagues in either a negative *or* a positive light are more likely to receive negative evaluations from supervisors.[6] Often, it is better to speak to people than about people.

Grow Your Insight # 32

Picture someone you admire and write down what you specifically admire about them. Are you inspired to share this information with others? How can this be done in a way that will inspire rather than create jealousy or opposition?

Insight # 33: Accepting a Compliment

Genuine compliments are words that build and inspire. Just as we accept physical gifts with grace and appreciation, we can also learn to accept compliments. For some people, this can be challenging. Notice how you feel or what you think when you are paid a genuine compliment. Do you make self-deprecating comments to deflect a compliment, or are you able to take complimentary words to heart?

Social praise on work evaluations improves human performance.[7] But, what happens in everyday life when receiving compliments from family, friends, co-workers, or acquaintances?

While it is believed by some that confidence is a prerequisite for accepting compliments, how is it that so many highly accomplished and famous people — speak honestly and vulnerably about their own feelings of recurring or perpetual self-doubt? Are they not accepting compliments and accolades for their achievements? I believe that it is possible for everyone to learn to accept a compliment, even without being completely confident or self-assured, and that by accepting this compliment, we are creating an opportunity to connect with its giver.

As I was working on writing this insight, there was a knock on my front door. When I answered, I found an elderly man asking for money. He comes door to door in our village each week in order to support himself. In an effort to connect, I asked him how he was doing.

He responded by mumbling something in Hebrew that I couldn't quite understand.

"What was that you said?" I inquired.

"Am I not speaking so clearly?" he responded.

"No, no… it's just that my Hebrew isn't 100 percent fluent. Could you speak a bit louder?"

"How long have you lived here?" he asked.

"Nearly four years," I answered.

"Your Hebrew is very good," he remarked.

And at that moment, a compliment and an insight landed on my doorstep. It was clear to me that I had two options. I could brush off what he said and disagree with him, discounting his opinion. Or, I could accept his compliment and acknowledge that standing in front of me is a person speaking in kindness and sincerity. Of course, I accepted the compliment, and for the first time in nearly four years, I saw this man smile.

In some respects, we are all walking around this world as humble beggars. We are looking to share value with a world which we hope can benefit from who we are and what we have to offer.

We are all teachers, and we are all students, and sometimes in the same moment. In the moment of accepting a compliment, we are accepting the value in a gift we are being given by someone else, and we are acknowledging the great value in its giver.

Grow Your Insight # 33

Look at yourself in the mirror, pay yourself a genuine compliment, and then accept that compliment fully.

Six

Peace is the Mission

Peace is the aim of Creation. The Torah itself is Peace, as it says:
"Its ways are pleasant, and all its paths are peaceful."
(MISHLEI, 3:17)

Jerusalem, 2003, continued…

Gazing out from the stairs leading down from my apartment and past a courtyard framed by loquat hedges, a sea of color filled my view. The street bordering our home had been transformed from its usual traffic artery into a blanket of bright, waving flags. Singing and chanting, hundreds … thousands of people filled the intersection and surrounding parkway.

Curiosity propelled me forward and down into the crowd.

Germany. Lithuania. Ecuador. China. Mongolia. Brazil. The flags were from every country imaginable, being held by people dressed in traditional garb from around the world. This was a convention of nations, and it was happening right outside of my kitchen window.

Who were these people, and why were they here?

What could possibly bring such a diverse crowd together, and how was it powerful enough to bring them all the way here... from nations across the globe, to convene in my front yard?

I meandered my way through a crowd of traditionally dressed Germans and met eyes with a heavy-set, broadly smiling woman. "We love you," she began. "We are here to express our solidarity with your mission of peace and your love for humanity. We are your partners in peace."

Taken by her immediate outpouring of affection, I felt tears welling up in the corners of my eyes. I asked her questions about this international convention of peace and love I had just walked in to. This was an annual gathering of people from around the world, convening in Jerusalem as a commemoration of an ancient Torah ritual.

In ancient Jerusalem, the house of Israel would perform rituals and prayers to invoke Divine protection, physical and spiritual prosperity would fill all of the nations of the world.

The ancient people of Israel believed that all of the nations of the world are destined to live in peace and harmony. Peace was their mission, inspired by the words of the Torah. Today, we carry that torch and we continue to believe that true peace is possible.

Insight #34 – Peace is another name for the Infinite

In our efforts to create peace, we can begin by focusing on the peace that exists within. By attuning our actions with our values, we can experience the peace of living authentically.

We may carry values even if we cannot consciously pinpoint what they are or why they are important. In coming to identify what we value, we can align our daily living to reflect what we care about most.

Within the framework of the Torah, the greatest value is righteousness. The highest compliment that one could receive is to be called "Tzadik," meaning just, fair, and right. Charity, in Hebrew, is not called 'charity.' It is called "justice." Giving a portion of earnings to those in need is a way by which a more just and peaceful world is built. That is the goal of the Torah, so much so, that one name for the Infinite is… "Peace."[1]

Self-improvement is a constant process. It begins with accepting that we need to change action. While this may seem self-evident, the ego goes to great lengths to justify its actions. Only in breaking beyond the ego's ability is it possible for a soul rectification.

The courage to have self-compassion and acknowledge that we can grow has the power to propel that growth itself and return us to the righteous nature within us and our deep, natural connection with the Infinite. Correcting an act and making this return can be likened to an estranged couple reuniting in marriage. Our essence is born to be at one with our Infinite nature, and when we return it is as though we are reuniting with that nature.

Grow Your Insight #34

To create a peaceful world, I believe that I need to…

Insight # 35: From Inner Critic to Inner Coach

The relationship between parents and children is the most influential and formative of relationships we can experience, beginning even before birth. We find a hint alluding to this in the ten commandments as they appear in the Torah.[2] The first five commandments pertain to humans and the Infinite. The second five pertain to humans and fellow humans (do not murder, do not be commit adultery, do not steal, do not bear false witness, and do not covet).

The commandment 'honor thy mother and father' is a notable exception, appearing within the first category although it is apparently between human beings. How can this be?

We learn that this commandment is actually in the correct category, between a human and the Infinite, because the spiritual level of one's parents is equivalent to that of the Infinite. In learning to relate to parents harmoniously, children are simultaneously cultivating a personal harmony with the Infinite.

Honoring one's parents, as it is explained, includes acts of serving food and drinks to them, standing in their presence when they enter a room, and not contradicting them. While standing in the presence of a parent or serving a parent may sound outmoded or outdated, acknowledging and prioritizing a parent's presence is timeless.

In taking a deeper look into psychological processes, we can understand the far reaching effects of honoring parents. Within the 'self-parenting' process, children come to idealize their parents.[3] Human beings begin self-parenting over the course of their development. This is the process through which a voice in the mind helps connect childlike hopes and desires with the adult self who has learned to function responsibly and set and achieve goals. If the inner child wants to act out in a moment of stress, the adult self steps in to 'parent' the inner child and offer a more mature response.

Learning to listen to the internal self- parenting voice is a byproduct from learning to listen to the parental voices in our lives. Optimally, parents who take their children's hopes and dreams seriously will inspire a self-parenting mechanism to grow within their children to acknowledge, celebrate, and nurture the creative, playful, idealistic inner-child dreamer.

Parents' speech and behavior toward children greatly influences how and what children think, even into independence and adulthood. Dr. Robert Firestone, an expert parenting psychologist, explains that naturally, "We parent ourselves the way we were parented in our family. This means that we tend to treat ourselves the way we were treated as children. If our parents treated us in a positive way, we will treat ourselves positively. If our parents treated us in a negative way, we will tend to treat ourselves in a negative way."[4] We can learn to develop self-love, self-care, and a more compassionate inner dialogue with an awareness of how we are parenting ourselves through life and an openness to change our beliefs about ourselves and about life.

There is a lesser-known Torah teaching which explains that honoring parents lengthens our days.[5] This lengthening may refer to a longer life, and it may also refer to simply living a better, fuller, more meaningful life. Children taught how to respect parents come to understand what being respectful looks like — they are taught to honor others, and they are taught that how they speak and behave matter.

As adults, we can notice our own thoughts and we can begin to formulate and develop a more loving, supportive, and even inspirational inner narrative.

Grow Your Insight # 35

Look at a photograph of yourself as a child. Offer this child your deep understanding, compassion, and encouragement. As you develop this voice, you can continue to speak to this child - your inner child - throughout the various stages of your life and into the present moment.

Insight # 36: Celebrating Responsibility

I nstituting responsibilities within our lives may or may not feel natural. Yet, recognizing and embracing responsibility is a mode of connecting with greater purpose.

Many people living today have been surrounded by the message that freedom from responsibility is what creates happiness. Marketing and advertising tout the benefits of relaxation and leisure.

Yet this notion that freedom from responsibility equals happiness is challenged by evidence to the contrary. This phenomenon of taking or shirking responsibility and its implications have been observed on a societal level in China, where traditionally, authoritative parents instituted a sense of responsibility *and* feelings of warmth within families, creating positive familial relationships.

Authoritative parenting was traditionally associated with well-behaved and academically successful children. In more recent years, since instituting a one child per family policy in 1979, Chinese parenting styles shifted dramatically. Parents indulged their only child more than previous generations had done, focusing their energies exclusively on this one child and requiring less from him or her by way of familial responsibility.[6]

The younger, only child generation has been observed as more selfish, egoistic, and lacking in gratitude than any generation prior. While the Chinese government has gone so far as to institute educational programming about morality and respect in order to correct the problem, the strongest predictor of respectful and well-adjusted children is an authoritative parenting style and not school-mandated programming. As of 2016, the one-child policy was eliminated.

We now understand that adolescents who value their role as helpers within a family show greater brain activation in the brain region directly involved with maintaining effortful control (dorsolateral prefrontal cortex).[7] In studies, even the young people who feel burdened by their responsibilities exhibit greater levels of happiness and positivity daily and an overall self-identification as "good" children. This attests to the tremendous value that children receive from taking responsibility in the home.

As parents, it's easy to fall into routines of caring for, and even serving children when they are able to perform these same tasks independently.

Yet, in considering the value of responsibility and its potential to influence brain functioning and overall wellbeing, we may realize that we are not burdening our children with responsibilities but rather helping to develop lifetime happiness habits.

Grow Your Insight # 36

How can we encourage an atmosphere of responsibility within our lives? How does / could responsibility add joy or meaning into your life?

Insight # 37 : Designating Time

One of the dramatic ironies of modern-day is that so many of the technologies designed to simplify our lives are allowing them to become busier than ever before. No matter how busy life can come to feel, by way of our awareness, we can channel our energy to live more intentionally, and even perhaps, more simply.

We are in the wake of a 'self-care' movement creating ripples in modern living, so large that the phenomenon has been deemed 'a millennial obsession.'[8] People are seeking help in prioritizing and structuring their lives, and in slowing down enough to take care of their primary physical vessels. We are spiritual beings living inside of physical bodies that need our attention and care.

From exercise to nutrition, personal coaching, meditation, healing modalities, and experiences geared toward wellbeing, younger generations are making their personal improvement commitments loud and clear.

There is a form of ancient self-care which is not being marketed along with the mainstream variety. It is a form of spiritual self-care which dwells in the sacred dimension of time. It is a designated time in which one declares 'I have created *enough* as of now, and this is the time in which I will simply *be.*"

It is the permission to take a break, rest, breath, and connect with oneself and others in a being-oriented rather than a doing and achievement oriented way.

It is a designated time to connect as human beings — despite where we come from, what we have accomplished, or what we 'own' — it is a time and place to recognize that we are all children of The Infinite One, and we can connect meaningfully, simply by letting ourselves be.

Whenever I'm trying to schedule a meeting and someone tells me that 'Saturday is family day,' or 'I don't work in the evenings,' I respect their decision to align their time with their values.

Devoting time in the day or a particular meal to be free from technology can be a sacred, designated time. Carving out dedicated time without distractions for solitude or for the people you care about are two ways to make the time more sacred.

In designating our time, we create peace in our lives. It is the peace of knowing we are devoting our time to that which is most important.

Grow Your Insight # 37

How can the concept of 'sacred time' be applied in your life? Where and when could you carve out time free from technology or entertainment to be alone or to connect mindfully with yourself or with others?

Insight #38 : Thinking Out loud

You may be one of the many people who love listening to podcasts, watching television, lectures, reading books, or attending live events. These activities are ways by which we immerse ourselves in the thoughts, ideas, and expressions of other people. Learning from others is one pathway to wisdom.

Listening to and learning from ourselves is the second, less traveled pathway to wisdom. Contemplate, for a moment, the ways in which you are immersed in your own thoughts and ideas.

Listening to your own voice has a tremendous power to connect you with your deeper self. This is a variety of self-care which provides the space for your inner voice and your soul can be heard.

Listening to ourselves think does not produce the same effect as listening to ourselves speak aloud. We each have a distinctly unique inner voice. By allowing ourselves the time and space to speak our minds out loud, or to pour our thoughts out onto paper, we are tapping into a deeper, quieter, and more peaceful place inside of our minds. We are clarifying our own perspectives and beliefs and becoming the master of our thoughts rather than allowing our thoughts to master us.

As the ancient sage Hillel once said: "If I am not for myself, who will be for me? If I am only for myself what am I? And, if not now… when?"[9]

The "I" is the deeper self which we are seeking to discover or develop, while the "me" is the persona which has been conditioned by its surroundings. In expressing your inner voice, you are connecting with the "I."

Grow Your Insight #38

Carve out a few minutes or more to listen to yourself speak, or take the time to write freely. Reflect.

Insight # 39: Finding Peace in Work

In Hebrew, the word for 'work' or 'service' is 'ah – vo – dah.' Interestingly, that same word 'ah – vo – dah' has a second meaning: 'worship.' Our work in this world — what we do with our time, both professionally and personally, can be viewed as our service to others, *and* part of our service to the Infinite.

While on the surface, work may seem to be the object of complaint and frustration for some, it can also be a source of tremendous satisfaction, joy, and purposeThere are tangible ways people find the most meaning in their work. Here are five:

1. **Challenge:** In his iconic research of what he calls 'Flow,' Mihaly Csikszentmihalyi asserts that enjoyment and creativity can be experienced through intense focus on work that presents challenges.[10] While people may be tempted or interested in finding a job that will be 'easy,' or 'mindless,' Mihaly's research indicates that satisfaction actually only comes from challenging work.

2. **A sense of progress:** In tackling challenges it is crucial to have a sense of making meaningful progress. Receiving help from others, respect, encouragement, and recognition foster a sense of progress.[11] In pursuit of a larger or more long-term goal, it's helpful to create smaller benchmarks to achieve along the way to notice and sense meaningful progress toward the ultimate end.

3. **Job Security:** In positions with a perceived high level of job security, an overall sense of satisfaction and purpose is much higher. Fear of being fired is not a motivator, and only creates an environment of negativity and dissatisfaction.[12]

4. **Freedom:** When given a choice between more money earned at a particular job or having more of a sense of autonomy in performing that actual job, perhaps surprisingly, it is the autonomy which leads

to more happiness. People will accept lower pay when given the opportunity to express themselves and speak more while working.

5. **Camaraderie:** The ability to develop and sustain meaningful relationships at work is a significant type of emotional compensation. While autonomy is important, collaboration and connection also play an important role in workplace happiness.[13]

Consider how work differs from slavery. Slavery has no constructive purpose. Slaves are not compensated monetarily for their backbreaking labor. Slaves in ancient Egypt, for example, were forced to build structures that were destroyed upon completion, demoralizing every effort as it was made. They were intentionally assigned tasks they were not designed for. Tall men with large hands were given delicate handiwork, and petite people were given heavy lifting. Without the opportunity to use their natural gifts and inclinations, the slaves were being set up for ongoing failure and frustration.

Our gifts and inclinations are our tools through which we build and shape this world. They have been bestowed to us in Infinite wisdom. With freedom and autonomy, work becomes our meaningful service. In every moment, we are free to focus our intentions on doing good work in this world. We can turn our attention to notice the fruits of our labors, we can share our creations and our abilities in exchange for value, and we can utilize our natural gifts and inclinations in all that we do.

Acknowledge your work as your service in this world, and your mind will be at peace and free to create.

Grow Your Insight # 39

How do you utilize your natural skills and abilities to do your work? Where do you notice that your work may have purpose and value?

Insight # 40 : Designating Time for Peace and Presence

I n the Torah's seven-day account of creation, the seventh day is distinct and separate from the other six. It is a commemoration of the day in which the Infinite ceased to create. When we consciously disengage from productivity in order to reconnect spiritually, we emulate this ceasing.[14] Disengaging from creativity is taking a step into the zone of time in which we can appreciate all that we have worked to create, and all that is provided to us through our surroundings.

When we designate time to simply be and enjoy, it can look like spending time in our homes, neighborhoods, in nature, alone, or with other people. Preparing a nice meal in advance and inviting family or friends to join in is a wonderful way to bring people together and designate a sacred time in our week.

My spiritual practice includes one full day of 'rest' from work each week. From Friday at sundown, the magic and power of rest envelop the next twenty-five hours. Phones, computers, and screens are powered off. Conversations shift into the here and now where we consciously celebrate time for having been created.

We taste delightful foods and drinks over lingering conversations. We share stories to inspire thoughtful dialogue. We sing, we connect, share ideas and reflections, and relish time for the sake of itself. With the goal of connection and enjoying the time, an ordinary moment can be made sacred.

I have found that this sacred time has brought an appreciation for simplicity into my life. Over the years, it has taken on different characteristics – some weeks there are more elaborate meals with guests, and other weeks are quiet and more focused on family, reading spiritual texts, taking walks, and reflecting.

One practice to try during a designated time – of any length – is that of consciously refraining from work and even discussing work. This is an opportunity to delve into other topics.

I have come to notice that after the designated sacred time concludes, I am able to return to the week of creating with renewed vigor, enthusiasm, focus, and clarity.

If we are looking for ways to discover and develop the more hidden parts of ourselves, setting aside designated time is one possible opportunity.

Grow Your Insight # 40

Visualize a sacred time in which you can pause from productivity. How does this look for you?

Seven

Cultivating our Connection

"Before you overthink, speak with Me."
—THE INFINITE

There was a certain gravity for me about stumbling upon the international contingency in Jerusalem – an immediately apparent magnetism. I realized that my purpose – our purpose – is to harness our unique, Divine gifts to make this world more whole, and ultimately, more peaceful. Each one of us, a fragment part, is longing to be reunified into a whole.

I had come to Jerusalem seeking clarity in the particulars of how to make my life meaningful, and on this morning, I came to understand that the particular was a vehicle to connect with the universal. All people have been infused with the breath of the Infinite, and as such, the best manifestation of my own life is one that aligns with the best manifestation for all of life.

Learning the truth, connecting with the Infinite, and living in service are ongoing endeavors taking on various forms as we grow and develop on our journeys. They remind us of our connection with depth both beyond and within this physical world. Each one of us can develop and grow our own unique, personal, and blissful relationship with the Infinite. Our acts of kindness are always in need, and each one of us has so much to offer.

Insight # 47: It's all (for the) Good

There are times when the forest of life may feel dense and dark without an inkling of light to be found. A small, still voice inside of us whispers that everything will be okay, but listening to this voice seems illogical. Is it unreasonable to have hope in times of despair? How can we know?

An ancient Torah morning blessing is recited as follows:

"Blessed are You…. (Infinite) … who gives the rooster understanding to distinguish between day and night." This appears to be a blessing of thanksgiving for the daylight, acknowledging the rooster that crows just before dawn. Before an inkling of light appears on the horizon hinting the forthcoming dawn… a rooster senses the sunrise.

Roosters remain in tune with the natural rhythm of the sunrise even when they are outside of their natural element and without exposure to natural light.[1] In Hebrew, the word for rooster is 'seckvi,' which is the same word for 'mind,' or 'insight.' Just as the rooster senses a forthcoming light when in darkness, our minds are endowed with the capacity to sense hope, even in the midst of despair.

'Emuna,' the Hebrew word for 'faith,' is a belief that we carry with us so deeply inside at all times; when life is going 'our way,' and even if life appears to be going a different direction. Emuna is the knowledge that even when we appear to live in difficult times, these too are ultimately for the good. It is the notion that there is a bigger picture in life which will ultimately make sense. We are a part of that bigger picture that our insight can sense even when our other five senses are unable.

On the Hebrew calendar, night precedes day. Darkness precedes light. We are endowed with not only the insight to differentiate between the two, but also the insight to know that the light will come. The light will come.

While we may not be endowed with the physical senses to predict or see the future, we can hold an awareness of a dawn in our mind. A present circumstance be experienced as an all encompassing darkness, yet the mindfulness of new horizons, a bigger picture, and a light at the end of a tunnel can wake us up to new possibilities.

Grow Your Insight #41

Have you ever been through a difficult time, and yet known on an intuitive level that something good could and would come from that? Can you reflect upon a challenging time in your life and notice anything positive that has come from this challenge?

Insight # 42: Our Deepest Expression

I n acknowledging the Infinite, we cultivate appreciation, awe, and wonder of That which has brought us into being and is sustaining us in all moments.

How can we express these deep feelings, and how can we utilize our thoughts, speech, and acts to connect with the Infinite?

When we focus our minds and hearts upon the Infinite and simultaneously tap into our deepest longings and most heartfelt appreciations, we are building bridges to channel spirituality into this world. Speaking to the Infinite is a quest to align the deepest depths of our minds and hearts to the most abundant, fair, peaceful, and loving Will that we can imagine.

These conversations have the power to peel back the veil of daily living and uncover concealed miracles. While initially, it may feel unusual to be speaking out loud and not to another person, speaking to the Infinite can be a healing, clarifying, and even enlightening practice.

We can speak to the Infinite as though It is an all-loving caretaker who loves us unconditionally, and has invited us to the most sacred and beloved of celebrations – life on planet earth.

As a human being subjected to systems of punishment and reward created and utilized by other humans to control your behavior and manipulate your experiences, you may feel challenged to transcend seeking approval and acceptance from others.

If you were conditioned as a child to relinquish authority to the adults in your life, as most children are, it may be difficult to hear and to acknowledge the voice of the Infinite that speaks from Within.

What were your dreams as a child? Were they taken seriously or were they laughed at? Were they nurtured or were they doubted? In recognizing the way that your childhood idealism was received by the authority figures in your life, you may come to an intellectual understanding of the way in which you approach the Infinite.

The past does not have the power to dictate your present, yet it may be able to provide you with the insight to recognize the ways in which your inner voice may have been put to sleep by your surroundings. If you can recognize how your Voice of Truth has been quieted, you can also visualize and create the surroundings in which it will be awakened.

In quieting the noise of your surroundings and beginning to speak to the Infinite who wants only to shower you with abundant blessings to fulfill your unique mission in life, you can awaken the Voice that has been sleeping.

We can pour our hearts out at any moment. The Infinite knows our thoughts. It knows our hearts. It is we who are working to awaken our own knowledge of It, and in our efforts to connect, we are moving closer to that knowing.

In pouring out our hearts, we uncover the pure seed and the voice of clarity which have been planted within us.

Grow Your Insight # 42

Speak to the Infinite.

What would you like to say?

Insight # 43: Serenity Beneath the Surface

Diving beneath the choppy ocean surface, we discover the calm and serenity of the depths. Quiet moments of contemplation and connection are personal gateways into the depths of our own minds and hearts. In a designated time and space, we can pull back the curtain of our outside orientations and tap into the wonder behind the scenes.

How will you greet The Infinite One?

In humility, one might begin with praise:

"Here I am walking along my path and I could be completely encompassed in where I'm going or the thoughts floating around in my mind, but I am pausing to have a conversation with You because You are the only True Perfection and I want to be connected with You in all moments.'

Just like speaking to the most loving and interested friend – a "Friend" that has no human qualities – I might speak about the beauty in the physical world— a cloudscape and its form and function within the ecosystem of nature, or a single flower and its intricacies, reminding me of the preciousness and complexity within even the tiniest of creations.

Speaking to The Infinite is a designated time and space to acknowledge what is already so right and wonderful in life - all of the people, places, things, and experiences that surround us. It is an opportunity to ask for anything - from healing, justice, peace, sustenance, energy, love, gratitude, or anything else that we believe to be optimal in this world.

The Infinite is Infinite and has the capacity to make anything happen.

Grow Your Insight # 43

How will you greet the Infinite? What would you like to express appreciation for? What would you like to ask for?

Insight # 44: All the Time in the World

A young man on his spiritual journey visited his teacher for advice. "How can I speak to The Infinite when I simply don't have time?" the student lamented. "What can I do?"

"Aaaah, yes. I have an answer, but it will take time to receive," replied the teacher.

"For you, my teacher, I have all the time in the world."

"Here is the time that you have just given to me. I am returning it to you so that you may pour out your contemplations and curiosities to the Infinite. Speak from the heart, and remember that you can always ask for more of anything that you need. Including time."[2]

Before we set out to do a spiritual act, it may feel as though there are forces are working against us, or that a particular inclination within the mind may be trying to lure us away. This can be especially true with embracing silence, quieting the mind, and connecting with The Infinite.

Focus on what is supporting you in your spiritual endeavors. What are the resources in your life that are encouraging you and assisting you to grow spiritually and connect in sincerity? These are the forces working in your favor, assisting you to open up a channel through which Divine inspiration can flow. There are always more forces helping you to do good than anything else, and in acknowledging their presence you will come to notice more of them.

We can practice speaking our hearts and minds out loud, and because we are human and face struggles, we can bring these into our conversations. Sitting down to consciously speak praises about this world has a way of putting my personal struggles into a clearer perspective. Speaking words of praise can bring about a sense of balance in our conversations with the Infinite and at any moment within the mind.

Making requests from The Infinite is an opportunity to ask for what we believe will be optimal for ourselves, for others, and for the world. Traditional requests include those for knowledge, understanding, intuition, repentance, connection, health, healing, prosperity, justice, forgiveness, spiritual enlightenment, requests of a personal nature, and others.[3],[4]

There are natural conflicts of the soul which may arise to your attention during your communion with the Infinite.

Some people may want to see a change and at the same time fear that change.

Someone praying for wealth may hold reservations about how money could bring added responsibility or unwanted outcomes into their life.

Someone longing for a life partner may be apprehensive about commitment, or fearful of the vulnerability required by a relationship.

Someone praying for health may fear losing the affection, attention, and support that has accompanied their illness.

Someone praying for their own material prosperity may feel guilt or shame for wanting more when there are so many others with less.

Awareness of these conflicts is the path to resolving them and living with inner peace.

We can remind ourselves that the Infinite is Infinite. Nothing is outside the ability of The Infinite One. Just as one candle has the capacity to light an infinite number of flames and lose nothing, The Infinite One has an unlimited capacity to bring healing, prosperity, and peace into this world.

While we may have come to believe that our prayers will be answered by way of the natural world and according to science or reason, these vehicles too have been created and are being sustained by the Infinite.

Which of the following are more miraculous to you: a human being carrying a one-thousand-pound boulder in one hand for a minute, or a human being carrying that same boulder for eternity?

You may believe that carrying the boulder for eternity is more miraculous, but if it is always happening, you could come to accept that this is not a miracle, but rather, science or nature.

This is the great miracle of science. We are being suspended in mid-air by a force that we call gravity, but it is no less miraculous than any person carrying a one thousand pound boulder.

Some people may believe that miracles are not real simply because they defy science or reason. When we realize that science itself has been created by a Miracle, we can reconnect with our natural sense of wonder.

Grow Your Insight # 44

Contemplate a natural creation or a scientific innovation.
Study its intricacies. Reflect.

Insight # 45 Visualization

In Hebrew, the word for 'believe' is 'ma-aa'meen.' This word shares the same root with the word "amen," an affirmation spoken after a prayer or a blessing, and with the word 'uman' which is an artisan or craftsperson. What is the connection?

Success in any area of life is the product of inborn gifts and abilities honed through deliberate practice.[5] As this is apparent in the arts, 'omanut,' it is also applicable to the ways in which we live our lives guided by our beliefs.

A belief is a thought experienced as truth. Our beliefs are the lenses through which we experience all of life, and the filter through which we generate thoughts, feelings, and actions.

The artist envisions a creation and physically manifests that vision into reality. The believer envisions an ideal with crystal clarity, and along each step of the way there, the believer notices the ways in which all of life is manifesting itself into that ideal.

There is tremendous power of belief and imagination in their ability to affect critical outcomes across disciplines. The practice of visualization increases the likelihood of a vision being manifested - a goal being achieved. [6]

An incredible story illustrates this idea. During a nine-year solitary confinement, political prisoner Natan Sharansky envisioned himself playing chess. He became so skilled at the game without ever actually physically playing, that he emerged from prison and beat the world chess champion in 1996.[7]

Visualization affects brain processes which mimic those of identical physical actions.[8] Similar to how memories or dreams can be experienced in the body as real events, future or imagined visualizations impact the mind and body in significant ways. The power of visualization has been studied in order to better understand its possible health implications. In one study, a group of volunteers wore arm casts for four weeks.[9] Half of the participants did mental visualization workouts of wrist flexing, and the other half did not.

After four weeks, the visualization group had fifty percent more wrist strength than the group that did nothing. Similar studies in the field of medicine continue to accumulate evidence that visualization of mental imagery can affect physical outcomes.

The power of visualization can be utilized in any area of our lives.

Grow your insight #45

Visualize yourself achieving a goal. Picture exactly what this looks and feels like. See yourself moving the individual steps along the path to the end goal.

Insight # 46 The Power of Belief

What we believe about ourselves influences how we live, and believing in our significance is an essential ingredient to being of service in this world. Rabbi Simcha of Bunim taught that "Everyone must have two pockets, with a note in each, so that he or she can reach into one or the other, depending on the need. When feeling lowly and depressed, discouraged or disconsolate, one should reach into the right pocket, and, there, find the words: "The world was created for me."[10] But when feeling high and mighty one should reach into the left pocket, and find the words: "I am but dust and ashes."

If we see a need in this world, we are seeing it for a reason. If we witness an emergency, we need to take action rather than relying upon someone else. If we are noticing an opportunity to assist other people by way of creating, innovating, or serving, it is because we have been provided with Divinely inspired insight, inspiration and opportunity to enhance the world.

Even the most accomplished people of all time have questioned their abilities. Believing that 'the world was created for me,' reminds us that our gifts and abilities have been bestowed upon us so that we can achieve our unique mission.

Grow your insight #46

How could thinking 'the world was created for me' motivate you to take action and believe in yourself more?

Insight # 47: What we (Actually) Need

O nce there was a businessman who traveled to visit the great Torah master known as the "Chafetz Chaim." The Chafetz Chaim lived in a humble abode in Radin, Poland. Taken aback by the minimalism of this great master's home, the traveler inquired, "Where is all of your furniture?"

"Where is all of yours?" The master replied with a question.

"I do not need any furniture because I am only passing through," replied the traveler.

"I, too, am only passing through this world," replied the master.

Y ou and I are spiritual beings living inside of a physical world. Our physical environment provides the framework through which we can fulfill our unique spiritual missions as we pass through.

In any moment, we can mindfully contemplate what it is we need in order to fulfill our purpose. We can ask ourselves about any object in our possession, "how is this useful in my life and how is it assisting me to fulfill my spiritual mission?"

Our physical surroundings can provide the optimal spaces for our deeper selves to flourish. In their form and function, our surroundings can imbue our lives with the elements which resonate most with our souls and inspire us to live our highest callings.

We can make peace with less, or we can make peace with more. Only you hold the barometer to gauge what it is that will best support you to be of service in your unique context.

If we are looking to acquire happiness by way of physical objects, we will always fall short. Yet, when we utilize physical objects in order to assist in our spiritual pursuits, the objects are thereby elevated to a spiritual level.

Recently, our family discovered that a nearby neighborhood had burned down in a forest fire. We felt immediately compelled to walk through our home to collect items to give away. A moment before hearing the news, we somehow felt that we needed everything in the house. Yet, hearing about the pressing needs of others and the opportunity to be of help far superseded our own sense of 'needing' all of our belongings.

More than we need things, we need to be needed.

Grow Your Insight # 47

Contemplate how your physical surroundings are assisting you to fulfill a spiritual purpose. How could you upgrade or modify your surroundings to better assist you?

Insight #48 - Our Need For Purpose

Abraham Maslow famously explained that human needs are hierarchical and that only after fulfilling the most basic of physical needs does one move on to seek fulfillment of the more complex emotional or spiritual needs. He proposed that only a small percentage of human beings would strive for self-actualization, meaning, and purpose over the course of their lives.

In 1943, as Maslow was refining this hierarchy, a twelve-year-old girl by the name of Edith was fine-tuning her ballet and gymnastic skills in Hungary. Abruptly, her country was invaded by Nazi soldiers and she was sent off to a concentration camp.

Upon arriving in Auschwitz, she and her mother met face to face with the infamous Dr. Mengele, known as the 'Angel of Death.' He asked young Edith, "who is this woman by your side? Is she your mother or your sister?" When Edith replied truthfully, her mother was sent directly to be murdered.

Today, Dr. Edith Eva Eger is ninety-two years old. She recalls this moment of her life in her recent book, "The Choice." She explains that she could have chosen to live emotionally imprisoned by this memory and the guilt surrounding having said the 'wrong' thing.

Yet, her mother's parting words, "no one can take from you what you have in your mind," resonated with her over the course of her lifetime, and inspired her to serve others even in her most desperate moments.

In Auschwitz, she was ordered to dance in front of the Nazi soldiers. As she danced, she imagined herself dancing in the Budapest Opera House. When she was rewarded for her dancing with extra bread, Edith selflessly chose to share these meek rations to save the lives of her friends dying from starvation. In turn, when she herself faced the imminent death of having to march miles and miles with a broken back, these same friends picked her up and carried her, literally saving her life.

Dr. Eger believes that we have the choice to be a victim or to be a victor. To be a victim is to be a prisoner of our own mind. In order to be a victor, we can find meaning in suffering and transform that suffering into an opportunity to discover the power within us.[11]

T he prison of the mind tries to convince us that our mistakes are powerful enough to limit our growth, and by way of guilt and regret it chains us to a story of the past. The mind may trick us into believing that we need to acquire our next possession or achieve the next professional milestone before we can make life meaningful and actualize our potential. Yet Dr. Eger's story and the wisdom that she imparts remind us that even in difficulty, darkness, and deprivation, we can *choose* to live a life of meaning and service.

Grow Your Insight # 48

Reflect upon your day and identify a moment in which you were given a choice to make that moment more meaningful. What was that moment, and how did you respond?

Insight #49 – It's Always a Good Time to Begin

One of the greatest Torah sages was Rabbi Akiva. Born in first-century ancient Israel, he was called a 'simple man' by way of his education and material means. At age forty, he began to learn the Hebrew alphabet and then the sacred texts. During his life, he disseminated Torah wisdom to tens of thousands of students. We learn from the life of this teacher that it is never too late to pursue our real passions and live our truths.

How can we set ourselves up for success and cultivate the mindset to support our goals? Every victory is the peak of a mountain that has been built from hard work, and most likely, a succession of failures.

We will never know what trials and tribulations have paved the pathway to the accomplishments of another person. When we contemplate our own past accomplishments, we can begin to see a clearer picture of success. We recognize that the hard work, learning, and obstacles that lined our paths were only there to sweeten the taste of victory in the end.

Only a small percentage of people who start writing a book or training to run a marathon will achieve their goal. Long term goals are more likely to be achieved when they are broken down into smaller, incremental milestones.[12] There is victory in each step of a process, and this knowledge in itself has the power to propel us forward.

Grow Your Insight # 49

What is one of your long-term goals, and how can it be broken down into smaller steps?

Insight # 50: Physical and Spiritual Meet

Contemplate the origin of any object and you will begin to uncover eternity. The pages of this book were processed from a tree. Its seed was planted from another's, watered by the rains in a water cycle that has been repeating since the beginning of creation.

It is beyond our human capacity to grasp the infinite nature of matter, and yet, we are within that infinite nature. When we place our awareness here, we peel back the veil of everyday life and become mindful of The Infinite Oneness beyond and within all things.

The Hebrew word for rain is "geshem." It is directly related to the word "gashmiut" which means "physicality" or "material". Rain is a great blessing which brings water to the earth and allows bounty to spring forth. Water is requisite for our very existence.

In Hebrew, the word for "sky" and "heaven" are the same: "shamayim." Just as rain falls from the sky, so too has everything physical been brought forth from a spiritual origin.

We ourselves are spiritual beings living in the physical world. It is our physicality which provides the vehicle for the depths of our souls' longings to be expressed.

Torah wisdom explains:

"A person whose wisdom exceeds his good deeds is likened to a tree whose branches are numerous, but whose roots are few. The wind comes and uproots it and turns it upside down. But a person whose good deeds exceed his wisdom is likened to a tree whose branches are few but whose roots are numerous. Even if all the winds of the world were to come and blow against it, they could not budge it from its place."[13] As we continue learning about and manifesting spirituality into the world, this metaphor of a tree is one we can engrave in our minds and hearts. We are living beings, deeply connected with all of life. With each breath, an opportunity to begin again. To heed the call of our soul. To remind ourselves of and to return to our purest nature, which connects us with all of life.

May we all be blessed to soak up the waters of wisdom and compassion, remain connected with our Source and ground ourselves firmly with acts kindness no matter how seemingly great or small.

Grow Your Insight #50

Final Reflection:

Review your forty-nine reflections.

How have your beliefs grown or changed?

How have your thoughts, actions,
and habits transformed?

Which new practices did you taste?

Which ones resonate for you?

Which insight would you like to revisit?

Afterword...

As I was in the process of writing this book, my very wise friend and mentor, Lib, asked me the following question: "If you were to write this book knowing that you will be the only one to read it, what would it be about?" This question guided me in writing 'Beyond all Things.'

I can say with candor that writing it helped me. I realized that in learning about and contemplating that which could enhance my own life, I was also learning about and contemplating that which could enhance the lives of others. As I began sharing excerpts, I received feedback that the insights were helping others to practice gratitude, live more joyfully, grow in self-love, and to perform acts of kindness. This was my inspiration to continue writing and to make this book widely accessible.

There is a tremendous joy I experience when I learn that my work has touched the life of someone else. I believe that we all experience such joy as we perform acts of service on this journey of life.

As an educator, I understand that an expert knows their subject best. It is also true that someone below the expert level may be better able to teach and explain parts of that subject to a novice, simply because of their proximity to being a novice. This is the reason why we can learn so much from our peers, and why students can educate one another in ways that a teacher may not be able. My intentions, in writing the insights, was not to espouse my personal mastery of spirituality, but rather my personal quest. For me, spirituality and the traits prized by Torah, are the work of life.

One of my own spiritual teachers in life, the Seventh Rebbe of Chabad Lubavitch of blessed memory, said that if we know one letter of the Hebrew alphabet, we can teach it to others. We need not master an entire subject and become an expert before we begin to teach parts of it. There is someone waiting and needing to learn the very thing that we are able to teach. Right now, *you* have so much to share with this world. This inspired me to write a book about spirituality and the value that it has brought to my life.

This book has been largely inspired by Torah. I revere and respect the Torah to the utmost, and wrote this book in order to share some of its wisdom with people whether or not they were previously familiar with the concepts it presents. I tried to make the writing inviting and inclusive to share the beauty I have found in Torah with the diverse and beautiful people I love to connect with so much. I did my best to convey Torah ideas in all of their splendor, and if I fell short in any way, it is not a reflection of the ideas or teachings themselves, but rather my own transmission. It is my prayer to continue to learn and teach Torah, for in it, we find the answers to all of life's questions.

This book was written with you in mind.

Every blessing to you now and always.

In Gratitude

Thank you to the Infinite One, abundant in kindness and mercy, for your ongoing guidance, love, sustenance, presence, and support in my life.

Thank you to my dear husband, Daniel, who exemplifies kindness. He is wise, creative, loving, a source of constant support and inspiration.

Thank you to my sweet children, Hana Aliya, Chaya Emuna, Avraham Yitzchak, and David BenTzion for being so lovable, loving, and showing me what present moment awareness looks like.

Thank you to my parents, Jim and Judy Farley, for being supportive in myriad ways.

Thank you to my parents-in-law, Dr. Joseph and Cathy Jankovic, for cheering me on with all of my creative projects.

Thank you to my wise friend, mentor, and writing coach, Libby Kiszner. You are changing lives with your work and with your words.

A special thank you to the early readers of this book whose feedback and inspiration guided me to finish strong: Yael Trusch, Dr. Madeleine Mejia, Adrienne Sholzberg, Chana Mason, Chaya Gross, Karen Vermeulen, Hillary Liber, the members of Circle of Insight community, my dear brother Benjamin Farley, and many others special souls - my friends and neighbors - You know who you are.

Thank you to Rabbi Dr. Yitzchak Breitowitz for reviewing this book, and for the thoughtful and insightful rabbinic guidance.

Thank you to the angels who surround me in all moments, in particular to my grandparents of blessed memory, Dr. Abe and Irma "Chaya" Golum, who inspire me to live with dignity, my dear Aunt Jill who inspires me to live with courage, my Grandma Jane Williams Farley who inspires me to live with kindness, and my great-grandmother Ella Sattinger Williams, my name sake, who inspires me to live with conviction to Truth. May your souls be uplifted to the highest of heights.

Thank you to my students for teaching me, and thank you to my teachers for seeing my potential. You know who you are.

About the Author

Azriela Jankovic is an educator, coach, and lifelong learner. She wrote 'Beyond all Things' and created SOULcare Coaching to empower the discovery and development of spiritual purpose and inspiration, with the ultimate goal of helping to increase peace in our world. In 2015, Azriela earned a doctoral degree in Education, focusing her research on the power of beliefs and relationships to transform and enhance lives. Together with her husband and children, that same year, she fulfilled a dream of moving to Israel where she gratefully resides with them today. You can learn more about SOULcare education initiatives and Azriela's upcoming seminars by visiting **AzrielaJankovic.com**.

End Notes

Introduction

1. Mitchell, Travis. "Young Adults around the World Are Less Religious." *Pew Research Center's Religion & Public Life Project*, Pew Research Center's Religion & Public Life Project, 13 June 2018, www.pewforum.org/2018/06/13/young-adults-around-the-world-are-less-religious-by-several-measures/.

Chapter One

1. "This Is Why Deep Breathing Makes You Feel so Chill." *Right as Rain by UW Medicine*, 4 June 2018, rightasrain.uwmedicine.org/mind/stress/why-deep-breathing-makes-you-feel-so-chill.
2. Genesis 2:7
3. *Division of Adam's Soul.* "Gate of Reincarnations": Chapter Six, Section 3, Beginner. By Rabbi Yitzchak Luria as recorded by Rabbi Chaim Vital; translation from *Sha'ar Hagilgulim* by Yitzchok bar Chaim; commentary by Shabtai Teicher
4. Hopman, Rachel & Scott, Emily & Castro, Spencer & Weissinger, Kristen & Strayer, David. (2017). Measuring Cognition in Nature - Neural Effects from Prolonged Exposure to Nature.
5. Yu, Chia-Pin, et al. "Effects of Short Forest Bathing Program on Autonomic Nervous System Activity and Mood States in Middle-Aged and Elderly Individuals." *International Journal of Environmental Research and Public Health*, vol. 14, no. 8, 2017, p. 897.
6. Kings I, 3:4-14.
7. Bigelow J, Poremba A. (2014) Achilles' Ear? Inferior Human Short-Term and Recognition Memory in the Auditory Modality. PLoS ONE 9(2): e89914.
8. "Listening: Our Most Used Communications Skill." *University of Missouri Extension*, extension2.missouri.edu/cm150.
9. Preston, S. D., and de Waal, F. B. M. (2002). Empathy: its ultimate and promixate bases. *Behav. Brain Sci.* 25, 1–20; discussion 20–71.
10. Headlee, Celeste. *We Need to Talk: How to Have Conversations That Matter.* PIATKUS Books, 2019.

Chapter Two

1. Excerpted from: https://breslov.org/joy-it-is-a-great-mitzvah-to-be-happy-always/
2. Christakis, Nicholas A, and James H Fowler. "Social contagion theory: examining dynamic social networks and human behavior." *Statistics in medicine* vol. 32,4 (2012): 556-77.
3. Conner, Tamlin S., et al. "Everyday Creative Activity as a Path to Flourishing." *The Journal of Positive Psychology*, vol. 13, no. 2, 2016, pp. 181–189.
4. Harvard Health Publishing. "Giving Thanks Can Make You Happier." *Harvard Health Blog*, Harvard Health Publishing, www.health.harvard.edu/healthbeat/giving-thanks-can-make-you-happier.
5. Nulman, Macy (1996). *The Encyclopedia of Jewish Prayer: The Ashkenazic and Sephardic Rites.* Jason Aronson, Inc. p. 125. ISBN 978-1568218854.
6. Attributed to Rabbi Menachem Mendel Shneerson of blessed Memory in s speech by Rabbi Manis Freedman https://www.youtube.com/watch?v=zn_9pJmrytY&t=289s. Retrieved July 4, 2019.
7. Malachim I, 2:7
8. Umberson, Debra, and Jennifer Karas Montez. "Social relationships and health: a flashpoint for health policy." *Journal of health and social behavior* vol. 51 (2010): S54-66.
9. Kumar, Amit, and Nicholas Epley. "Undervaluing Gratitude: Expressers Misunderstand the Consequences of Showing Appreciation." *Psychological Science*, vol. 29, no. 9, 2018, pp. 1423–1435., doi:10.1177/0956797618772506.
10. Dewall, C. Nathan, and Roy F. Baumeister. "From Terror to Joy." *Psychological Science*, vol. 18, no. 11, 2007, pp. 984–990.
11. Rabbi Kalonymous Kalman Shapira, The Piasetzna Rebbe, *Derech HaMelech.*

Chapter Three

1. A. Ito, Tiffany & Larsen, Jeff & Smith, Kyle & Cacioppo, John. (1998). Negative Information Weighs More Heavily on the Brain. Journal of Personality and Social Psychology. 75. 887-900.
2. "Loss Aversion: Behavioraleconomics.com: The BE Hub." *Behavioraleconomics.com | The BE Hub*, www.behavioraleconomics.com/resources/mini-encyclopedia-of-be/loss-aversion/
3. Ethics of Our Fathers, 4:1
4. Newswire, MultiVu - PR. "New Cigna Study Reveals Loneliness at Epidemic Levels in America." *Multivu*, www.multivu.com/players/English/8294451-cigna-us-loneliness-survey/.
5. Stellar, J. E., Gordon, A., Anderson, C. L., Piff, P. K., McNeil, G. D., & Keltner, D. (2018). Awe and humility. *Journal of Personality and Social Psychology, 114*(2), 258-269.
6. Zenger, Jack, and Joseph Folkman. "The Ideal Praise-to-Criticism Ratio." *Harvard Business Review*, 27 June 2017, hbr.org/2013/03/the-ideal-praise-to-criticism.

Chapter Four

1. Based on the commandment 'Love your fellow as yourself,' as it is written in Leviticus,19:18
2. Maimondes, Laws of Personal Development, 4:1.
3. "The Problems with Nutrition Science." *Dr. Mark Hyman*, 5 Feb. 2018, drhyman.com/blog/2018/02/01/problems-nutrition-science/.

4. TED Talk: Suzuki, W. https://www.ted.com/talks/wendy_suzuki_the_brain_changing_benefits_of_exercise?utm_campaign=social&utm_medium=referral&utm_source=facebook.com&utm_content=talk&utm_term=science

5. Naumann, Earl. *Love at First Sight: the Stories and Science behind Instant Attraction.* Sourcebooks, 2004.

6. Acevedo, Bianca P., et al. "Neural Correlates of Long-Term Intense Romantic Love." *Social Cognitive and Affective Neuroscience*, vol. 7, no. 2, 2011, pp. 145–159.

7. Based on the work of Carol Dweck: Dweck, Carol S. *Mindset: Changing the Way You Think to Fulfill Your Potential.* Robinson, 2017.

8. Ethics of the Fathers, 2:10

Chapter Five

1. "Four-in-Ten Rural Residents Know All or Most of Their Neighbors; Shares Are Smaller in Urban, Suburban Areas." *Pew Research Center's Social & Demographic Trends Project*, 15 May 2018, www.pewsocialtrends.org/2018/05/22/what-unites-and-divides-urban-suburban-and-rural-communities/psd_05-22-18_community-type-00-13/.

2. Butler, Robert N. *The Longevity Prescription: the 8 Proven Keys to a Long, Healthy Life.* Avery, 2011.

3. Genesis 49:12

4. Van Edwards , Vanessa. "You Are Contagious." TedX, London. Retrieved from https://www.youtube.com/watch?v=cef35Fk7YD8

5. Anderson, E., et al. "The Visual Impact of Gossip." *Science*, vol. 332, no. 6036, 2011, pp. 1446–1448.

6. Grosser, Travis J., et al. "A Social Network Analysis of Positive and Negative Gossip in Organizational Life." *Group & Organization Management*, vol. 35, no. 2, 2010, pp. 177–212.

7. Sugawara, Sho K., et al. "Social Rewards Enhance Offline Improvements in Motor Skill." *PLoS ONE*, vol. 7, no. 11, 2012.

Chapter Six

1. Talmud, Shabbat (G-d's name is Peace)

2. Deuteronomy, 9:15

3. Firestone, Robert, et al. *Creating a Life of Meaning and Compassion: the Wisdom of Psychotherapy.* American Psychological Association, 2003. Pp. 62

4. Firestone, Robert. personal communication via email on March 20, 2019.

5. Deuteronomy 5:16

6. Li, Shi, and Sims, Margaret. (2018), Developing Gratitude and Filial Piety: The Role of Chores. In: Education Quarterly Reviews, Vol.1, No.2, 168-174.

7. Fuligni, Andrew J., and Eva H. Telzer. "Another Way Family Can Get in the Head and Under the Skin: The Neurobiology of Helping the Family." *Child Development Perspectives*, vol. 7, no. 3, 2013, pp. 138–142.

8. Silva, Christianna. "The Millennial Obsession With Self-Care." *NPR*, 4 June 2017, www.npr.org/2017/06/04/531051473/the-millennial-obsession-with-self-care.

9. Ethics of Our Fathers, 1:14

10. Csikszentmihalyi, Mihaly. *Flow: the Psychology of Optimal Experience.* Harper Row, 2009.

11. Kramer, Teresa and Amabile, Steven J. "The Power of Small Wins." *Harvard Business Review*, 8 June 2016, hbr.org/2011/05/the-power-of-small-wins.

12. Miana, Beatriz Sora, et al. "Consequences of Job Insecurity and the Moderator Role of Occupational Group." *The Spanish Journal of Psychology*, vol. 14, no. 02, 2011, pp. 820–831.

13. Gallup, Inc. "Item 10: I Have a Best Friend at Work." *Gallup.com*,26May1999.www.gallup. com/workplace/237530/item-best-friend-work.aspx.

14. Designated time, while inspired by the traditional 'Sabbath,' is not intended as a replacement for ritual, traditional Sabbath observance. It is merely a Sabbath-inspired suggestion for anyone looking to explore taking time 'off' in a different manner.

Chapter Seven

1. "Cock-a-Doodle-Doo: No Need for an Alarm Clock: Highlights." *Nagoya University Academic Research & Industry-Academia-Government Collaboration*, www.aip.nagoya-u. ac.jp/en/public/nu_research/highlights/detail/0000906.html.

2. Story adapted from a Torah class given in person by Rabbi Elchanon Tauber of Los Angeles, California, USA. A sample collection of his teachings can be accessed online at https://www. youtube.com/channel/UCgiuG9Slj4deKiw8FTU9ebA

3. On making personal requests in the traditional order of prayer see Peninei Halacha: https:// ph.yhb.org.il/en/03-12-10/

4. On the eighteen benedictions of the traditional Torah prayer service https://www.chabad. org/library/article_cdo/aid/3834226/jewish/What-Is-the-Amidah-The-Silent-Prayer.htm

5. Ericsson, K. Anders, et al. "The Role of Deliberate Practice in the Acquisition of Expert Performance." *Psychological Review*, vol. 100, no. 3, 1993, pp. 363–406., doi:10.1037/0033-295x.100.3.363.

6. Cheema, Amar, and Rajesh Bagchi. "The Effect of Goal Visualization on Goal Pursuit: Implications for Consumers and Managers." *Journal of Marketing*, vol. 75, no. 2, 2011, pp. 109–123., doi:10.1509/jm.75.2.109.

7. Miller, Michael. "Russian Immigrant Minister Beats World Chess Champion." *AP NEWS*, Associated Press, 15 Oct. 1996, www.apnews.com/92b1c4c794e1493c3ef427da8f237714.

8. Yao, Wan X, et al. "Kinesthetic Imagery Training of Forceful Muscle Contractions Increases Brain Signal and Muscle Strength." *Frontiers in Human Neuroscience*, Frontiers Media S.A., 26 Sept. 2013, www.ncbi.nlm.nih.gov/pmc/articles/PMC3783980/.

9. Ranganathan, Vinoth K., et al. "From Mental Power to Muscle Power—Gaining Strength by Using the Mind." *Neuropsychologia*, vol. 42, no. 7, 2004, pp. 944–956.

10. Mishnah Sanhedrin, 4:5

11. "Dr. Edith Eva Eger: The Choice" SuperSOUL Conversations, Harpo Productions, Apple Podcasts, June 16, 2019, http://www.oprah.com/own-super-soul-sunday/dr-edith-eva-eger-the-choice

12. Bandura, A., & Schunk, D. H. (1981). Cultivating competence, self-efficacy, and intrinsic interest through proximal self-motivation. *Journal of Personality and Social Psychology, 41*(3), 586-598.

13. Ethics of our Fathers, 3:22